China's Leaders

IN IDEAS AND ACTION

China's Leaders

IN IDEAS AND ACTION

Cornelia Spencer

MACRAE SMITH COMPANY : PHILADELPHIA

ACKNOWLEDGMENTS

The author wishes to thank the following publishers for their kind permission to reprint the poems and quotations used in this book: Poem on page 25 from *The Importance of Living* by Lin Yutang, The John Day Company, Inc.; poem on page 50 from *The Rise and Splendour of the Chinese Empire* by Réné Grousset, University of California Press; poem on page 54 from *A History of Chinese Literature* by Herbert A. Giles, copyright 1901 by D. Appleton and Company, renewed 1928; poems on pages 65 and 66 from *Oriental Civilizations: Sources of Chinese Tradition* by William Theodore deBary, New York, Columbia University Press; quote on page 163 from *Portrait of a Revolutionary* by Robert Payne, Abelard-Schuman, Ltd. Copyright year 1950.

Contents

1: *Confucius (551–478 B.C.)*   7
   CHINA'S MOST FAMOUS MAN

2: *Ch'in Shih Huang Ti (259–210 B.C.)*   20
   CHINA'S FIRST EMPEROR

3: *Wang Mang (33 B.C.–A.D. 23)*   31
   CHINA'S FIRST SOCIALIST EMPEROR

4: *Hsuang Tsung (A.D. 686–762)*   42
   THE EMPEROR WHO LOVED THE ARTS

5: *Wang An-Shih (1021–1086)*   50
   PRACTICAL POLITICIAN

6: *Hung Hsiu-Ch'uan (1812–1864)*   59
   LEADER OF THE TAIPING REBELLION

7: *The Empress Dowager Tzu Hsi (1834–1908)*   72
   CHINA'S GREATEST WOMAN RULER

8: *Sun Yat-sen (1866–1925)*   95
   FOUNDER OF THE CHINESE REPUBLIC

9: *Generalissimo Chiang Kai-shek (1886–   )*   115
   LEADER OF EXILED NATIONALIST CHINA

10: *James Yen (1898–   )*   136
    ORIGINATOR OF THE THOUSAND CHARACTER
    MOVEMENT

11: *Mao Tse-tung (1893–   )*   149
    LEADER OF THE CHINESE COMMUNIST
    REVOLUTION

12: *Chou En-lai (1898–   )*   168
    PREMIER OF RED CHINA

    Bibliography   189

Pronunciation Guide

Ch'in Shih Huang Ti	chin she WHO-ANG DEE
Wang Mang	WONG MONG
Hsuang Tsung	shoe-ANG dzung
Wang An-shih	wong an-she
Hung Hsiu-Ch'uan	hoong she-oo chu-AN
Tzu Hsi	TSOO SHE
Sun Yat-sen	soon yaht-sen
Chiang Kai-shek	chee AHNG KY-SHECK
Mao Tse-tung	mau dzu-doong
Chou En-lai	JOH EN-LIE

China's Leaders

IN IDEAS AND ACTION

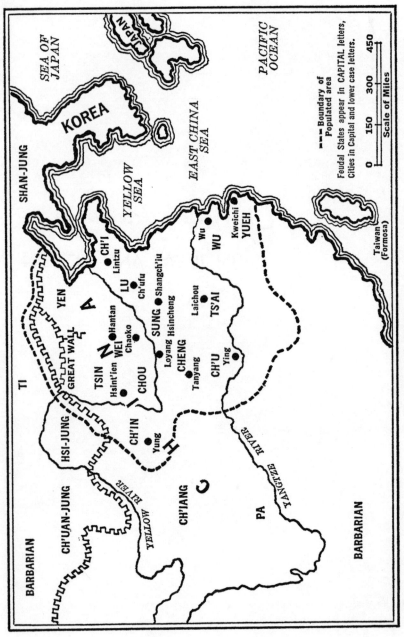

China at the Time of Confucius

1

551–478 B.C.

Confucius

CHINA'S MOST FAMOUS MAN

The man pictured to us as Confucius in ancient sculpture, or on watercolor scrolls, usually sits with his hands crossed and tucked into long sleeves, his gentle face topped by a scholar's cap, lost in thought. One bronze image in a Confucian temple in Tokyo, Japan, brought there by a Chinese exile many years ago, shows him almost smiling, while two definitely buck teeth show above his lower lip and flowing beard. Accounts say that he was an unusually tall man though here he looks rather round-shouldered and small. Perhaps that is only because his full, flowing robes, those of ancient China and not the trim ones of today, lie in deep folds across his chest.

Confucius lived a long time ago and records about him have either grown dim with age or have glorified him until it is hard to find out just what he was really like. We do know that he was probably the most important Chinese thinker who has ever lived because of his influence on history. His ideas dominated the Chinese for more than 2,000 years.

Confucius was born in 551 B.C. when China's mainland was broken up into several feudal states which had never been united into one nation, though groups of them, kingdoms, had come and gone. Confucius lived during the middle of China's second period of recorded history, the Chou, which was to last almost a thousand years. He was born in the village of Tsou, in a small feudal state called Lu near the seacoast, now the Shantung Province.

The best record of Confucius' life that we have is in *Shih Chi* or the *Book of History,* written by China's first great historian, Ssu-ma Chien (148-85 B.C.), who lived almost 400 years after Confucius. His name will appear again because his account is so important. Ssu-ma Chien was especially interested in finding out about Confucius because China's first emperor, who had tried to stop the spreading influence of the teachings of Confucius by burning his books, was dead and people were bringing out copies they had hidden away. Scribes were busily making more copies for Confucius' ideas were more popular than ever. Ssu-ma Chien had to find out for his own satisfaction just what it was that made this ancient teacher's theories so hard to destroy.

He began his search in Tsou but was told conflicting stories about Confucius' background. Asking for what records there were, he studied them and discovered that Confucius came from a family with the name K'ung, once considered nobility, who had lived in Lu, part of the kingdom of Chou. When the Lu throne had fallen into the hands of dukes to whom it did not belong, the K'ung family fell upon hard times and became very poor and unimportant.

Confucius' mother was a young woman whom his father had either taken as a second wife, which was quite proper in China at that time, or whom he had simply become interested in when he was already sixty-five. His father died when Confucius was very small and too young to ask any questions. His legal mother, his father's first wife, never told him anything about his true mother. The first wife even kept his father's place of burial a secret from him. This mattered a great deal to him when in a few years she died, too, and he had to have her buried with his father. The people of the Chou kingdom worshiped their ancestors and proper burial was important. Finally, a woman in the village admitted that she knew that his father lay buried in his own village. At last Confucius was able to have the burial carried out as it should be.

By the time he was fifteen, Confucius was determined to get an education, for he loved books. He must have enrolled in the village school where students memorized ancient literature, learned about religious ceremonies, how to worship clan ancestors properly, and how to take part in festival rites. But to have respect for one's elders was the most emphasized teaching.

While the other pupils probably were only interested in learning how to behave and be accepted by the adults in their families, Confucius seemed to have a higher purpose. Later he said, "Even in a hamlet of ten houses, there will always be one whose loyalty and reliability is the like of mine, but there will be none who loves learning as I love it." He liked to read the ancient books, written in lacquer ink on lengths or slips of bamboo and tied together. The *Odes,* poems and songs sometimes sung with accompanying instruments, and the *Documents* excited him. Even when Confucius just read them it was like music for he had to read them aloud in order to give the words their proper tones.

One time he had a chance to hear the *Odes* sung beautifully when an orchestral group of blind master musicians came from the Chou kingdom capital. Confucius listened to them in delight. After that he always had a special feeling for blind people and offered them his seat and bowed to them, even though they could not see him. His friends teased him about it.

Although Confucius was on the way to becoming a scholar,

he was also a poor boy and an orphan. He had to work as well as study. For a while he kept books as an accountant. When he was seventeen one of the Lu barons hired him to be in charge of his granary, his cattle, and his sheep. Confucius did this work so well that the baron found a political position for him, although it was not a very important one.

During this time Confucius was also trying to decide what to do with his future and trying to discover what life was all about. Poverty he knew about from his own experience and all around him people were sick and suffering. He could not keep from noticing cruelty and meanness and unfairness, too. Wealthy families who had seized the power in his own state did not care what happened to their subjects as long as they had their own comforts.

Confucius began to dream of a political career. If anything were to be changed it would have to be changed by the government. He wanted to help get his state's royal line back on the throne again. If only he could get into a high political position he could use his influence to clean up the government and depose the usurpers. The records of Ssu-ma Chien show that other young men were beginning to gather around him to listen to him discuss his ideas.

One story tells of Confucius and one of his disciples asking the Duke of Lu if they might go to the Chou capital, the present Lo-yang, a great distance away, to study the performances of rites and ceremonies. The Duke furnished them with a carriage, horses, and even a coach boy or page, and they set off on their journey. The tale goes that they met the famous philosopher Lao-tze in the capital and that he gave them some advice. The philosopher would have been much older than Confucius and greatly experienced and full of wisdom, but most historians doubt whether the two young men ever reached the distant capital, much less ever saw Lao-tze.

Confucius could not decide which was the best way to influence government. His small political job soon ended and he found that one did not just walk into politics. Time passed while he waited for some opening or until he thought of some other way of changing things. In 517 B.C. the authority of the Duke of Lu was challenged by a rebellion led by two other noble families. When he lost the fight and had to take refuge in a nearby state called Ch'i, Confucius loyally followed him there.

The state of Ch'i was bordered by the sea on two sides and its capital was much more exciting than any town in Lu. There Confucius heard ancient music performed in a way that charmed him. Later he wrote about how he felt: "I did not reckon that the beauty of music could reach such a pitch." The orchestra that performed the music was far better than the amateur musicians at home.

Although the music of the Ch'i people was wonderful, Confucius gradually found that their politics were worse than those in Lu. In 509 B.C. he decided that he had been away long enough for he was now almost forty years old. He returned to Lu.

The next ten years were bad ones for the state and for Confucius himself. A dictator named Yang Huo was now in control and began trying to persuade Confucius to enter politics. Confucius tried to evade him because he knew that this man only wanted to use his abilities and his good reputation to improve his own position.

Confucius was living in the Lu capital now and Yang Huo sent him an invitation to come for an interview. Confucius refused it. Then the dictator sent him a pig as a gift and again invited him for an interview. Confucius had to be polite and go to the court to thank him, but he carefully chose a time when he knew that Yang Huo would not be there. Confucius set out but the two accidentally met in the street!

Yang Huo said, "Come, I wish to speak with you. Could

it be called an act of 'humanity' to possess such a valuable
jewel as you have, and cheat the state of it?" He knew that
Confucius was always talking about showing humanity and
kindness to others.

Confucius answered, "No, it cannot."

Then Yang Huo went on, "Can one who, in spite of a desire
to serve in office, is forever failing to grasp his opportunities
be called a wise man? Time is slipping by."

Confucius could only say, "Very well: I will accept the
office."

He took the government post unwillingly and historians
have wondered why he did it at all, unless he was simply
caught in Yang Huo's net of words. The man he had to serve
now was an enemy of the rightful rulers. He was one who
Confucius had wanted to depose. He was opposed to all that
Confucius believed in, that was why he could twit Confucius
about his humanity.

In 501 B.C., when he was fifty, Confucius became the
mayor of a town. At fifty men automatically had a certain
status in the community. He made his town into a model city
and was selected to represent Lu at a peace conference in
another state. It was a great affair and he met representatives
of many other regions. Confucius' popularity grew quickly
after this. In 499 B.C. he was promoted to the position of
Minister of Crime, a high office, and became an important
person.

Now, at last, in this position he hoped to bring about some
change in the rule of his own state. He started to plot ways of
deposing the usurping wealthy barons and of replacing them
with the authentic ruling line. It seemed that he could work
best by getting his own men into more and more important
offices. This might lead to actually weakening baron strong-
holds, even tearing them down. He finally recommended his
most brilliant militarist friend for a high post, but by now the

barons questioned his intentions. They suspected that Confucius was dreaming of using his office to overthrow them because he believed in the cause of the common people. He lost his office when they were sure of what he was trying to do and it was a great blow to him. He decided to leave his state and travel. It was 497 B.C. and he was already fifty-four years old.

Confucius did not come back to his own state for thirteen years. During that time he wandered about among the other states of the Chou kingdom, surrounded by a group of disciples. Everywhere he went he found that people had heard of him because of the peace conference he had attended. Scholars also knew of him because of his ideas of society. He and his disciples were invited to the courts of one state after another. When their carts or carriages arrived, they found important men gathered to listen seriously to Confucius' ideas on government and social organization. He drew them out, too, and collected information about their states and about their citizens. The long trip turned into a kind of political crusade because of his ability as a speaker. People liked to hear his unique ideas; they liked the way he talked.

Princes of these other states also wanted to listen to Confucius because they knew that he had tried and still wanted to bring about a revolution in Lu so as to put back the rightful heirs to the throne. They were curious about him. But while they received him as an important guest and listened to him excitedly, they did not pay much attention to his purpose. They were very comfortable as they were and they had no wish to upset things. His ideas were unusual and original and fresh, but they did not take him seriously enough to consider him dangerous.

Confucius visited small states first but when they seemed deaf to changes he was suggesting, he decided to visit the more powerful ones. He began to think that perhaps he was a man of destiny, that is, perhaps Heaven had chosen him to bring a better day to his people. The Chinese way of saying this is that he had a "mandate from Heaven." Gradually, he felt so sure that he had this mandate that he did not believe anything or anyone could hurt him and so interfere with Heaven's will. His disciples, too, believed that he had been chosen for a special mission. They stayed with him year after year, traveled with him, and gradually grew old with him. A time came when the youngest among them was thirty; the oldest over sixty. But the larger and more powerful countries which they visited did not pay any more serious attention to Confucius' ideas than the smaller ones had.

One day, looking around at all of his disciples as they came to rest in the shade of a clump of trees, Confucius realized how he loved them. How faithful they had been! It did not seem right for him to let them go on wandering about the countryside for a cause which he saw now would never be achieved while he lived. He decided that it was time to go home. He would spend the rest of his life in teaching and writing.

Why had these men wanted to follow him as pupils all these years? What made them unwilling to leave him even when he did not find any prince who would accept his ideas? Perhaps he could not have answered these questions himself. It may have been that his way of teaching attracted them above all else. He did not lecture them; he did not argue his points. He did not even do most of the talking. He knew each man personally and they had conversations, as friends. Confucius led his pupils into thinking about things. New ideas came, new answers, and the disciples found the experience of following him one they did not want to give up for anything else.

Confucius had developed his own methods of teaching and they were revolutionary ones for his time. He said, "The superior teacher guides his students but he does not pull them along; he urges them to go forward and does not suppress them; he opens the way but does not take them to the place." "A good questioner (teacher) proceeds like a man chopping wood—he begins at the easier end, attacking the knots last, and after a time the teacher and student come to understand the point with a sense of pleasure."

Confucius was not interested in religion, nor was he superstitious as many ancients were, but he was interested in relieving the suffering of people. He did not have curiosity about the supernatural for he approached ideas almost like a scientist, reasoning them out, and did not like to spin out theories about life. Instead, he opened up human problems, problems which people had to solve, and tried to suggest practical answers for them. He described his approach clearly when he said, "Virtue is to love men. And wisdom is to understand men." He thought of the family as the unit, the smallest complete part of mankind. The nation was a larger family with the emperor as its father. All the peoples of the earth were children of Heaven. One of the most quoted of his sayings still is "All under heaven are one family."

Confucius had a faith in humanity as a whole, not just in special individuals. This faith was unusual in ancient times for it was taken for granted that education was only for the few and that only some men were important. Confucius was revolutionary in declaring that while everyone did not have the same amount of ability, all, regardless of their backgrounds, should have a chance at education so as to become good citizens. He proposed a system of examinations which any boy could study for and take in order to qualify for a government position. These civil service examinations became famous as time passed because they were unique for their time in history. Confucius also said that government ought to be a cooperative affair and that everyone ought to take part in it. This was surprising talk for his day when autocratic dukes, powerful only because they were wealthy, were doing whatever they liked in his own state.

Confucius dared to disagree with popular points of view, and he dared to act in unusual ways. Even in small things he was often like this. He liked to fish but he would not use a net, only a rod. He liked to hunt with a bow and arrow, but he would not aim at a bird at rest. People thought he was ridiculous but he insisted that both of these things would be unfair to the animals. He was what we today would describe as an individualist or an original thinker.

Confucius liked to talk about what he called *li*. He meant keeping things in order among people, having proper relationships between people from the emperor down to the smallest child or the least important servant. He believed that the basis of a better society must be made up of two things—love for one another or the Golden Rule, and respect for authority. He loved rites and ceremonies because, if they were properly carried out, they were a sign of the orderly grouping of people in a society, each performing its part. He loved ancient poetry and music and dance because they represented disciplined relationships between people.

He loved music just for itself, too. He learned to play on a stringed instrument called the *ch'in* and often accompanied his own singing. When he was sixty-four he edited the *Book of Odes,* a collection of songs and ballads which had come from past ages. He said some things about music which may make us stop and think. "Music comes from the inside, while ritual comes from the outside. Because music comes from the inside, it is characterized by quiet and calm . . . Truly great music is always simple in movement, and truly great rituals are always simple in form. When good music prevails, there is no feeling of dissatisfaction, and when proper rituals prevail, there is no strife or struggle." "When you see the type of a nation's dance, you know its character."

While Confucius thought that everyone ought to have a chance at education, and while he believed in genuineness or honesty, and while he loved the real arts and while he emphasized the Golden Rule, he still hated some qualities in people. He told one of his disciples, "I hate those who spy on others and think that they are clever. I hate those who think they are brave when they are merely unruly. And I hate the wily persons who pretend to be honest gentlemen." "I hate the goody-goodies because they confuse us by seeming to be the virtuous people."

Confucius died when he was seventy-two. He is called the founder of Chinese literature as well as the person who influenced China's history more than anyone else. He loved to study ancient writings and bring them together in an organized way. Because of this it is difficult to know what he himself wrote and what he took from others. He edited three of the *Five Classics*. The first was the *Book of History* coming from sources reaching from 2400 to 800 B.C. The second was the collection of poems and ballads in the *Book of Odes*. It is thought, too, that he gathered the material for *Spring and Autumn Annals,* a history about the state of Lu between 722 and 484 B.C. The title really means all four seasons, or all time, for spring includes summer, and autumn includes winter.

The *Analects* is a short version of his books and is one part of the *Four Books* which every Chinese student used to have to study. No one would have thought of trying to begin on the *Five Classics* without first mastering the *Four Books,* and so the Confucian *Analects*. This meant that the ideas of Confucius became the background of Chinese education and thought.

It is easy to see that because Confucius was a unique person and one who used original ways of living and teaching, students might like to gather around him and even stay with him for

years on end. We can understand that he wanted to bring rightful rulers back to power. We may admire his ideas of government and of the good society, but it may still be hard to see why
his influence was as great as it was. Perhaps it was because his
teachings became the basis of the moral system of Confucianism which developed after his death.

Confucius' theories of education were followed for 2,000
years. They stressed good behavior, the Golden Rule, order,
and right relationships within society, and connected all these
ideas with ancient books. While Confucius had explored those
ancient books for their true meanings, after his death much of
the vitality of his ideas was lost because he was no longer there
to interpret them. Confucian education gradually discouraged
exploration and discovery by becoming rigid and following
very strict rules. Still, his system of civil service examinations
went on generation after generation. Boy after boy passed
through them to high office in the government or perhaps just
to being an honored scholar in his hometown. It still did not
matter what class of a family he came from so long as he could
pass the test. But the material on which the examinations were
based had lost the inquiring touch of Confucius and became a
mass of information to be memorized and to be preached
about in long essays.

Confucian ideas of government were retained, too. The nation should be like a great family with the emperor at the head
and each member in his place. The ruler should be kind and
everyone beneath him should be considerate of others also.
Although the plan of government was kept, people did not
always live up to its high standards. Officials were often
chosen from among those who had passed the civil service
examinations but who did not have the other good qualities
they needed. Like the examination system, the form continued
but the human qualities which Confucius had intended to
strengthen and emphasize gradually disappeared. What was

left was a formal organization tightly controlled at the top. Confucius' philosophy which had started as a search for the meaning of life, for the best way for people to live with each other, with a government that would emphasize the human side of life, gradually changed into the dead forms of Confucianism.

Through the centuries, Confucianism conditioned the Chinese people to accept the authority of those over them, to obey their elders and to follow certain rites. No great national change came until the Chinese Revolution of 1911. The Revolution failed and after many troubled years Russian Communism came into China and found a people who had rebelled against the Confucian ideas of empire and were discouraged in their hope of becoming a republic. Before they knew it they were taking orders again from someone who told them what to do, for these orders promised them a better day. If Confucius had been there he might have said, "If a ruler desires what is good, the people will become good also. The character of a ruler is like the wind, and the character of the common people is like grass, and the grass bends in the direction of the wind." "When the ruler himself does what is right, he will have influence over the people without giving commands, and when the ruler himself does not do what is right, all his commands will be of no avail."

2

259–210 B.C.

Ch'in Shih Huang Ti

CHINA'S FIRST EMPEROR

Millions of people from all over the world have gazed in wonder at China's Great Wall which stretches across her northern frontier. Miles of it still stand as strong and beautiful as when they were built two thousand years ago. The rest of it remains as a huge embankment marking a course over high mountains and deep valleys. Why was it ever built through a countryside that looks so calm and peaceful? What enemies were to be kept out by it? And how was it built at a time in history when men had no machines?

The man who built the Great Wall was Prince Cheng who lived about three hundred years later than Confucius. Until the reign of this prince, China had never been unified and was made up of many unorganized parts. Among these, three feudal states showed themselves stronger than the rest. They fought it out among themselves in bloody war, not hesitating to behead thousands of their captives for it was a ruthless time in history. The state of Ch'in won over the other two and Prince Cheng became heir to its throne in 247 B.C. when he was a boy of thirteen.

Prince Cheng's story begins with his father who was a

prince of the Ch'in state, in exile because of the wars. He had a friend, a merchant, who wanted to get the prince back to his rightful place and hoped, at the same time, to improve his own position in the state. The merchant at last succeeded in bringing the prince back to his capital, only to have him fall in love with his own wife. It was a difficult situation, but in order to promote his own advancement, the merchant gave up his wife to the prince and Prince Cheng was born to her.

When the boy of thirteen took his place on the throne at his father's death, the merchant became his prime minister. Although he was not royalty and no scholar, he had succeeded in his dream of advancement. He served his prince well and was the first commoner to hold such a position in China's history.

By 234 B.C. Prince Cheng was ready to take action. One of his counsellors described him as "a man with a prominent nose, large eyes, the chest of a bird of prey, the voice of a jackal, and the heart of a tiger or wolf." He soon began to act in ways that matched his looks.

First he sent out his armies against the other feudal states, determined to conquer them and unify the country. He succeeded in doing this by 221 B.C. and the name China comes from this first unification into an empire under the state of Ch'in. Prince Cheng now renamed himself Ch'in Shih Huang Ti, or First Emperor of the Ch'in Dynasty. Before this time rulers had been called *wang,* or king.

With an empire rather than warring states to deal with, Shih Huang Ti could begin to organize the government. He wanted to demonstrate some of his ideas for he was full of dreams and plans.

First of all, to do away with the boundaries of the old feudal states, he decided to redivide the empire. He would make it into forty provinces or political units, subdividing these in turn into much smaller counties. Each province would have its military governor, its civil administrator, and its supervisor who would report directly to him. The Emperor was careful to choose for these positions men who were from the governing class, and men who were friendly toward him. Thus he would have tight control over them. With this done, he thought over the political system with satisfaction. It was new and it was well organized.

Naturally, not everyone was as pleased as he about these sweeping changes. The old feudal leaders were upset by them, but they were afraid to complain openly and they did not find a chance to plot secretly against the Emperor. He had them all—thousands of them with their families—moved to the empire's capital, Hsien Yang, near Ch'ang-an later called Sian. There he could rule over them and there they also served a useful purpose. They created a market for luxury goods for they were accustomed to living well. Fine craftsmen and merchants flocked to the city and it grew and became prosperous.

Now that he had worked out a political system for his empire and had taken care of the opposition, Shih Huang Ti began to think about other reforms. Many different peoples were under his rule now and they had no common spoken language. Only a few could read, even fewer could write, and not even a common written language existed. Something had to be done about the annoying situation and the Emperor turned to a scholarly friend, Li Ssu, for advice. Li Ssu had come from one of the other states and was a Legalist, or one who believed in close organization of government and tight control from the top. Already he had been helping the Emperor with political planning. Now he set his mind on the problem of seeing what to do about a written language.

Li Ssu adopted a simplified form of characters which had already been used by one of the small states, added to it and standardized it. One would want to make writing as simple as possible since it had to be done with a bamboo stylus, or pen, and lacquer ink on lengths of bamboo. A great many of these slips, about nine inches long and only wide enough for a single column of words, had to be tied together to make a book. When Li Ssu had worked out a standard style of writing, he also selected a word list. This list was sent out all through the empire and was China's first dictionary.

Although it is difficult to be sure of dates, many historians believed that the Chinese began to write on silk instead of bamboo about this period for the hair writing brush was invented during this time. Inventing the hair brush was much more important to the Chinese than it may seem to us today for it soon led into the whole field of Chinese watercolor art and Chinese writing art, or calligraphy, which are famous all over the world. The brush could express rhythm and emotion in writing as well as shades of color in painting. The brush also started the search for something to replace silk—paper.

Ch'in Shih Huang Ti had to standardize other things beside writing and word lists if he wanted his empire to work efficiently. All sorts of weights and measures were being used; sometimes each merchant in a town had his private set. Constant quarrels and fights resulted, especially when the tax collector came. Something had to be done about it so the Emperor himself chose systems and declared them standard. They were, he decreed, to be put into use throughout the land. A good many heads shook and a good many deep sighs were drawn and there was secret muttering over the decree, but no one dared disobey it.

Still another problem grew more and more pressing because of the increasing traffic in and out of the capital. Oxcarts and wagons traveled in wheel tracks rather than over the whole road. When axles were of different lengths the tracks they made were irregular and broken. Roads grew worse and worse. The Emperor did the only thing that could be done— he decreed that all axles were to be the same length.

But this question of axles brought up the whole business of

roads. Shih Huang Ti began to think it over. Why not build a system of new roads—broad, paved ones that any chariot could roll over and any cart run on? The idea appealed to him and he started to build roads radiating out of the capital in all directions. The roads were quite magnificent—fifty paces wide, raised where they might be flooded, and bordered by trees.

Constructing roads led to still other projects. He had a splendid palace with a mausoleum built for himself. It was not finished until two years before he died, but that is easy to understand because of its huge size. It was 2,500 feet from east to west and 500 feet from south to north. Ten thousand people could assemble in it. Standing opposite the main part of the city, it was approached by a broad thoroughfare bordered by beautiful and interesting attractions. Scattered in the outskirts of the city were many imperial residences which were connected with the palace grounds by covered or by walled roads.

As time went on, Shih Huang Ti thought of yet other ways to improve communications. Many canals crisscrossed the countryside but some of them were no longer navigable because they had filled up with silt. He had these dredged and deepened. He employed Li Ping, a man whom we would call an engineer, to work out an irrigation system for a rich part of a western province, now Szechuan. Li Ping cut a pass through mountains so that a river could flow into a system of canals and made a great area flourish.

The Emperor thought of many of these reforms because he kept traveling over the country himself and saw what was needed and checked on how his orders were carried out. Travel was slow, by chariot, by oxcart, or perhaps sometimes by horseback, but he knew how his plans succeeded.

On his travels he noticed sections of high wall here and there, that had been built by feudal lords to protect their estates. The country still needed protection along the northern border for while his armies had defeated a militant tribe called the Hsiung Nu, he suspected that they might attack again someday. There would always be a threat to the north and it might as well be prepared for. He started to build a great barricade against such an invasion—the Great Wall. Using forced labor—conscripted laborers—as had been used for the road building and canal-clearing, the long fortification slowly took shape as old portions were saved and strengthened and new sections were built.

The wall snaked its mighty way across the landscape. At last it reached from the shore of the North China Sea, or the Yellow Sea, to a point a thousand miles inland. About one half of that length was new. The wall was from 15 to 50 feet high, depending on the terrain, and 15 to 25 feet wide at the base, narrowing a little at the top. Stories of how cruelly the hawk-nosed emperor's officers treated the laborers have come down through history. Although these stories may have exaggerated the truth, it is more likely that they tell only part of it. Not only were the laborers beaten and driven to do their work, heavy taxes had to be imposed to pay for it. A poll tax was collected, and even salt and iron were taxed.

Dr. Lin Yutang, a well-known modern Chinese writer, mentions one of the many stories that grew up among his people about the building of the Great Wall. It is said that a widow, whose husband Mengchiangnu had died of hard labor while working on the Wall, cried so much over his bones that her tears washed away a section of it. He quotes, too, a ballad about Shih Huang Ti which the Chinese people often recited or sang, depicting the emperor as a tyrant.

> *Ch'in Shih Huang is going to die!*
> *He opened my door,*
> *And sat on my floor,*

He drank my gravy,
And wanted some more.
He sipped my wine,
And couldn't tell what for:
I'll bend my bow,
And shoot him at the wall.
When he arrives at Shach'iu,
Then he is going to fall!

Although the first emperor of China is pictured as a brave, cruel, domineering man full of great plans and mighty ambitions, he had other surprising sides to him. He was often afraid. He was afraid of how people who hated him might treat him, and he was even more afraid of spirits of the unseen world. Sometimes he slipped around in disguises because he feared he might be assassinated. He was terrified of dying and was highly superstitious.

In order to insure his own safety, one of the first things he did after he came to the throne was to confiscate all weapons except those that belonged to his own forces. He had them melted down and cast into bells and monuments. Then to offset this confiscation and make the people happy, he decreed that peasants could own their own land. This was a great change from the feudal system and it pleased the people.

But Shih Huang Ti remained afraid. Somehow he must control thought, he decided, so as to check criticism of his rule. This step was to lead him into an act which would make him as infamous as the building of the Great Wall would make him famous.

During the Chou Dynasty, the time of Confucius and other outstanding philosophers, thinking freely, discussing, arguing, learning from great minds, and writing about any subject, had become popular. Shih Huang Ti now decided that this freedom might be dangerous to him. Li Ssu's theories of autocratic control and close organization of the government were beginning to result in whispers of criticism; and some also appeared in the form of memorials or written messages to the court. The scholars were reading Confucian non-Legalistic writings, it seemed. They would make the people critical of him and he wanted to check this tendency before it went any further. He asked Li Ssu for advice. Li Ssu came up with an astounding plan which would remove all danger of past ideas and would also let the First Emperor start his own history of China. He suggested that all existing books be burned.

Shih Huang Ti decided to carry out this drastic plan. He decreed that local officials must confiscate official chronicles of feudal states, the oldest book of poetry, the *Book of Odes,* the oldest history, the *Book of History,* and all the discourses of the philosophers. The only books spared were to be copies of these which were kept in the imperial library and all books about agriculture, trees, divination, and medicine. Books were still made of bamboo so when they were burned it must have been quite a bonfire. But even after they had been destroyed scholars kept remembering long passages from the ancient classics and talking about them. The Emperor angrily ordered that anyone caught discussing them from memory would be executed and his sons would be sent into exile. Hundreds of Confucian scholars are said to have been executed by being buried alive.

Perhaps it was possible to control one's subjects but it was next to impossible to do much about spirits and the unseen world. There seemed to be no way to avoid dying and entering into that world one's self. Shih Huang Ti kept looking for some elixir of life, something that could magically keep him from death. Meantime, he did everything he could to conduct himself properly with the spirits. He held great assemblies when as emperor he made sacrifices to the gods with elaborate ceremonies. There were five gods to be thought of, representing the five elements—fire, water, earth, air, and metal—and the five directions—east, south, west, north, and center—as well as the five planets. But although he did all this with the greatest pomp, he was still uneasy. If he overheard anyone speaking of funerals or death he grew angry and ordered that it should never happen again. In his palace he had several sleeping rooms kept ready so that no one would know in which one he was on any particular night. He studied the stars carefully before he made any decision, and yet he was afraid that something would happen to him.

Someone told him that there was a magic drug which would make a person immortal. Who knew what it was? Immortals who lived in the sacred mountains, he was told. So he set out to visit the sacred mountains in the islands off the coast to find out about this precious substance, accompanied by a group of 500 girls and 500 young men. The young people never returned and some say that the islands of Japan were populated in this way. Perhaps this story also has another meaning. Perhaps it shows that Shih Huang Ti was anxious to enlarge his empire even more and used this way of doing it.

Shih Huang Ti had moved northwest and pushed back the Hsiung Nu before he built the Great Wall. He had reached down into the Korean peninsula and set up his authority there. In 221 B.C. he sent his armies southward and in two years' time the Ch'in empire reached as far in that direction as what is now Hue in South Vietnam. He populated the countries with people who had nothing to do or with criminals. But although he had done all these things, although his empire now stretched in all directions, he was still afraid of age and death. He went on looking for the elixir of life and many of his trips were part of this search.

In 210 B.C. he went on a long journey accompanied by Li Ssu, but he took the precaution of making sure that if anything happened to him the throne would go to the elder of his two sons. He sent his son a message saying that whenever he died his son should come at once and accompany the body of his father to the capital and conduct the funeral ceremonies properly as an heir to the throne should. But Shih Huang Ti did not know that Li Ssu had secretly plotted against him and changed the message so that it ordered the son to commit suicide on the death of his father. This was part of a conspiracy to have the second son assume the throne.

Shih Huang Ti died on that journey, at Shach'iu as the ballad mentions. Li Ssu knew that if the death of the Emperor were known the people would rebel against the dynasty and its succession. He had to keep the Emperor's death secret. On the return journey of the great imperial cavalcade he managed to hide the fact that the royal chariot bore a dead body rather than a living man. So it came again to the capital without anyone knowing that the Emperor had died. Since the first son had obeyed his father's order and taken his own life, the second son conducted the funeral, and assumed the throne before the people had time to protest.

The proper funeral ceremonies over, the body of Shih Huang Ti, who had been only fifty years old, was taken to his mausoleum. Its location was a secret and few knew what it was like inside. A hundred years after the Emperor's entombment the great historian Ssu-ma Chien described it in his *Historical Record*. Situated on Mount Li, filled with rare objects and costly jewels, it was guarded by mechanical crossbows which would discharge arrows at any intruder.

The Second Emperor felt that any of his father's wives who had not given birth to sons ought to accompany the dead monarch to the next world, so many perished at the time of the funeral. As the workmen who built the sarcophagus knew of its location and the treasures it contained, once the internment was complete, the entrance was blocked so that not one of them escaped.

Ch'in Shih Huang Ti had not been able to conquer death though the great empire of China had come to being under his rule. A strong man, tyrant, leader, and conqueror; people called him a Chinese Caesar, a Superman, but in his heart of hearts he was always afraid.

3

Wang Mang

CHINA'S FIRST SOCIALIST EMPEROR

Two hundred years after the time of Ch'in Shih Huang Ti, the builder of the Great Wall, the power of the Han Dynasty was interrupted suddenly by a man who was full of original ideas. From a family of commoners named Wang, with the given name Mang, Wang Mang stepped into history as dramatically as an actor who appears before the footlights of a stage to entertain the audience while the scenes are being shifted behind the curtains. The Han Dynasty would continue in power after his act was over, just as it had gone on before him. Wang Mang could interrupt the drama of the Han Dynasty because the royal heirs had grown weak and poor in their leadership.

The story of Wang Mang begins with a young woman of the Mang family who was chosen by one of the princes as his second wife. She was pleased to be chosen and her luck continued when she gave birth to a son, providing the throne with an heir. When this boy was nineteen his father, then Emperor, died and the woman from the Wang family quickly stepped forward as Empress Dowager. She kept a strong hand on the court and when her son had ruled for twenty-five years and died without an heir, she again acted promptly. Since the only person who could claim the throne was a small boy of nine, she looked about for someone she could put into real authority, for she was now old. If the Wang family were to continue its power she saw it would have to be through cunning, for it could not claim to be of royal blood.

She decided on Wang Mang, a nephew with a reputation for Confucian scholarship, good personal behavior, and simple living, as Regent for the boy Emperor. Wang Mang took his place as Regent and for some months played that part. Then, mysteriously, the boy Emperor became ill and died. Rumors whispered that he had been poisoned.

Wang Mang acted with caution for he felt his own ambition swelling. There stood the throne, empty, but he must not move quickly. After all, he was a Wang and not of the line of Han. History paints him as gifted, dramatic, odd, genuinely concerned for the people, and with extraordinary ways of thinking and behaving. All these sides of him appeared as time went on.

For three years Wang Mang made no move toward assuming the throne, but then he prepared to make himself Emperor. First of all, he set out to convince the people that he had had been chosen by Heaven and that he had been given a mandate from Heaven to set up a new dynasty. In the *History of the Former Han Dynasty,* which was completed in the first century of the Christian era, we read of the strange ways Wang Mang used to prove this fact.

The signs that proved that he had a mandate from Heaven, he told the people, were clear. The state of Annam (now part of Vietnam) had sent him a gift of a live rhinoceros. Heaven had provided him with a three-colored horse, an iron certificate, a stone tortoise, an image of a mythical beast, a tablet of dappled jade, a dark dragon, a sacred well and a silk chart. He claimed that each of these events had special significance.

When he had experienced twelve such signs that he should become Emperor, he had a vision. It was of a man who told him specifically that the mandate of Heaven was being passed from the Han Dynasty to him. When word of this vision was circulated the officials of the court held a great meeting and while they were discussing what to do next, a statue spoke and said, "You must urge the Emperor of the Hsin (New) Dynasty to go to the Temple of the Han and receive the mandate."

What more needed to be said? Wang Mang had a large number of copies of this account of what had happened made and sent over the countryside. It was proof enough that he had a right to the throne. But still, to make doubly sure, he took another step. He worked out a family tree for the Wangs which traced his ancestry back to a great mythological figure called the Yellow Emperor who it was said ruled about 3000 years B.C. This took him back much further than even Confucius and rooted his place in history in the channel which would carry him through the Chou period when Confucius had lived. Now he felt he had certainly proven his claim to the throne. He had succeeded in doing something else, too, and that was to glorify Confucius himself. All the stories about The Master were repeated and connected with Wang Mang's work in creating a family tree, starting a new emphasis on the teaching of Confucius. Wang Mang soon appeared as an authority on Confucian literature and also seemed to have been approved by that ancient teacher.

In A.D. 9 Wang Mang at last declared himself New Emperor or Emperor of the New (Hsin) Dynasty and began making all the reforms he had been dreaming of. Conditions were poor and he had theories of how they ought to be improved. The question of landownership was always important in a farming country and Wang Mang began with it. Land had gradually been collected by leading families until most of it was owned by only a few landlords who rented it out to farmers, charging in payment far too large a proportion of their harvests. To correct this Wang Mang nationalized all farmland and redivided it so that each farmer had what he considered a fair share.

Slaves, both men and women, were owned by those who could afford them and Wang Mang saw how cruelly they were treated. He declared an end to slavery but such a roar of protest went up that he had to withdraw his declaration. The next thing he attacked was the wide range of prices for ordinary goods. Prices varied so much that people suffered many injustices. Wang Mang had a survey made and then declared what he felt were fair asking prices. He also had the government buy up food surpluses and hold them so that they would be on hand in case of famine which so often swept over the country. Then hoarders could not ask people to pay prices that were far too high, or else simply starve. He looked into the question of debts. In order to meet the costs of weddings and funerals, families took on terrible weights of debt which they had to pay back at usury rates. Wang Mang arranged a system of state loans which people could get to carry them through these major expenses. He continued existing government monopolies on salt, iron, and coinage and added monopolies on wine and all mines.

Wang Mang did something else which perhaps no one else would have dared to do. Perhaps he dared to only because he was certain that he had a particular responsibility and a peculiar ability to meet it, for an odd thing had begun to happen to him. He had begun to really believe that he had a mandate from Heaven; that all the propaganda he had created to justify his seizure of the throne was true—all the messages, events, and mysterious visions were fact. Taking it for granted now that Heaven had chosen him, he moved forward with assurance. Now he decided to change the coinage, bringing in all gold and substituting bronze.

Whether he had any idea what a widespread effect this was going to have, one can only guess, but the result was that China's trade was paralyzed. Her trade had been great under the Han Dynasty, reaching as far West as the Roman Empire. Under Wang Mang's edict the Roman Emperor Tiberius before long declared that no Roman citizen should wear Chinese silk because it was bought with Roman gold. The Roman women loved the silk which was finer than any other material they could get for their flowing dresses; it was smooth, cool, and clinging. Silk was easily carried across the great overland distances. Now everyone had to give it up because of the curious usurper of the Chinese throne. In Ch'ang-an, the capital, the gold piled up and bronze coins went out. History would call Wang Mang a counterfeiter and a miser.

While he was intent on these many government matters and genuinely interested in improving conditions, he had another major project on his mind—to put in order the records and the histories of the past for the generations yet to come. Engaging a scholar named Lui Hsin, the work on ancient literature began. Lui Hsin first prepared an enormous catalog of all existing writings, often called China's first bibliography. Others were engaged to help in what became a very large undertaking. Texts were copied and edited; some authorities say they were also added to or changed to please Wang Mang.

Wang Mang wanted to revive the interest of the Chinese in the teachings of Confucius. He is also known as the emperor who restored the literary cult to the high position it had held during the Chou Dynasty during the time of Confucius. He so idealized that ancient period of history that he glamorized it for others, especially for young men who were interested in glorifying their country.

Wang Mang built great dormitories to house thousands of students who came to study in the libraries he was improving. In the capital he repaired a temple to Confucius and students flocked there to read inscriptions cut in the stone tablets of the walls and to burn incense to the memory of The Master. Confucius was not regarded as a god and his teachings were not a religion, but they came nearer to this than they had ever before. As still another touch, Wang Mang bestowed a special honor on a descendant of Confucius who lived in the city.

In some ways Wang Mang resembled Confucius—he too was an original thinker, he too was anxious to reach underlying ideas because only they seemed important. Wang Mang had wanted to bring a better day for the country by having a better man on the throne. Confucius had tried to restore the princes of Lu to the Lu throne. Wang Mang seemed to have decided that there was no acceptable Han prince and so had taken the throne himself. Perhaps Wang Mang went even further than Confucius for he believed so strongly in his theories of government that he worked at them almost day and night, asking nothing for himself and living so simply that he scarcely seemed to be an emperor. The ideas he implemented were not always his own for among the scholars who clustered around him were men with socialistic dreams which he adopted and modified. During these years when he was still a young man, his fame went out and reached across Europe.

Whether or not people liked what he proposed, they at least found him interesting. Those who came to see him found him bent over his records, or in audience with those who had come to complain, often white and drawn with fatigue and with no interest at all in display or show. He was not an ivory-tower scholar, withdrawn from realities, lecturing a group of followers. He was a man of ideas and the heart of his thinking was that the lot of the average citizen must be improved.

This was a revolutionary idea! He was shaking the whole structure of society, taking away the lands and the slaves of the wealthy, buying up the surpluses which the officials hoped to use for personal profit when famines came, as they so often did, and meddling with coinage so that trade was almost paralyzed—and all for the unheard-of idea that peasants and middle-class merchants had their rights. But none of the growling against his changes disturbed Wang Mang who was as sure as ever that the original ideas of Confucius were like his, and that most important of all, he, Wang Mang had a mandate from Heaven to carry out his plans.

When Wang Mang reached the age of sixty, he could no longer pretend that there was no trouble on the country's horizon. This time he realized that he had foolishly brought it on himself. So as to trace everything back to the Chou Dynasty and wipe out the Han, he had ordered all the Han Dynasty ancestral shrines which were scattered through the villages destroyed. This desecration aroused a strong Han clan named Liu. Two of its leaders openly opposed Wang Mang. They met and said, "Come, we will join together and find others who are sick and tired of this usurper and we will go against him in strength." They did not have to look far to find followers. Secret societies are among China's oldest organizations. Now one of them, called the Red Eyebrows, came forward, eager to help.

The Red Eyebrows had been born during a time of natural disasters. About 3 B.C. a dreadful drought had come to an area which is now part of Shantung Province, northeast of Ch'ang-an. Thousands of starving people began to wander in search of food, praying to the gods of their fields as they went. Seven years later, before the country had begun to recover from this terrible event, the Yellow River, which flows through the province, broke its dikes because of heavy rains and flooded the surrounding lands. A leader arose and organized the peasants, ordering them to paint their eyebrows red as a sign that they were his followers. The Red Eyebrows became a strong secret society and found support everywhere because more and more people turned against Emperor Wang Mang. In A.D. 18 the Red Eyebrows were at the head of a real rebellion against him.

But Wang Mang did not seem to be disturbed even when a

courier came running one day with the terrifying news that the Red Eyebrows were marching toward Ch'ang-an. It all seemed remote from what he was trying to do. He had his mandate from Heaven. The people who had tried to be loyal and help him even though they did not always understand him, now began to desert him. Some of them suggested that he had better escape while he could, but he brushed them off, his mind not on what they said. Days passed and more rumors came.

A faithful friend visited him and said with tears in his eyes, "Lord, tens of thousands of starving peasants are marching on the capital, and still you will not listen! Reports are that they are killing the officials in all the towns they pass through. It is rebellion, sir, rebellion!"

Wang Mang looked up from his books and said mildly, "Then I shall order the imperial troops to go out against them."

"What can imperial troops do with men who are starving," his friend murmured, sadly. "They could not hold back the barbarians on our northern borders," he added and then wondered whether he should have brought that up. The barbarians had broken over the northern borders in recent years and Wang Mang had shown none of the ability of the builder of the Great Wall in holding them back. He had seemed scarcely interested.

Now Wang Mang looked up, but as if from a great distance, and said under his breath, thinking aloud, "Ah, those barbarians." It was true he had not remembered in time how important it was to hold that northern line.

"And who can make the people of Annam send tribute as they once did—remember the living rhinoceros?" his friend went on, daringly and cruelly.

Ah, yes, Annam. He had not thought much about countries to the south, either, and as for the rhinoceros—well, he would not press the point. He had been too busy strengthening the central government and reviving Confucian scholarship to bother with less important things.

The friend left and found others lingering anxiously in the shadows. "It is no use," they whispered as they slipped away.

Wang Mang ordered the imperial troops out against the rebels and then he put the matter from his mind and returned to his theories of state.

In ten days a courier came bringing such bad news that his face blanched as he fell before the Emperor. "The rebels are approaching the capital. They are only one long day's march away."

"Where are the imperial troops who were sent to stop them?" Wang Mang asked.

"They have disappeared. Some say that they have joined the enemy," the courier panted, wiping his face with a shaking hand.

Wang Mang suddenly remembered that he had once heard that the forces he had sent against the northern barbarians only joined them, too. But he felt nothing serious could happen to the capital and to him. He dismissed the courier and returned to his work.

The next morning another courier came to report. The bloodshed was terrible. Whole villages were wiped out or joined the great army sweeping on toward Ch'ang-an. They were led by two Han princes named Liu, helped by the Red Eyebrows. It would be only hours; perhaps before the sun set they would be at the city gates.

Wang Mang listened and if he understood he gave no sign. When the man had finished, he waved him away and then said to a servant, "See that the poor man is rewarded."

The day wore on. The city grew deathly still. Merchants hid their goods. Women were disguised to look like men. The old were made into beggars who stood shivering with fear at the street corners. It was as if a terrible plague had wiped out half the population. But in the palace Wang Mang would not let anything be changed. He worked as usual.

In the late afternoon the same faithful friend who had tried to warn him before appeared at his elbow. He dropped on his knees. "Sir, they are at the very gates of the palace and will you still not even try to escape? Will you wait here and let them cut you down?"

"Do you not know that I have a mandate from Heaven and that none can hurt me?" Wang Mang answered. "But you— you must not sacrifice yourself for me. Go hide in that chest under my bed and when they have gone I will myself come and release you."

"Oh, Friend," the man said rising quickly, "you will never come and release me for they are coming now. At least go to the tower in the garden. There you will die as befits an emperor, in the place which masters the whole palace." He turned and ran. Only seconds later a great shout went up and Wang Mang knew, though he did not wish to know, that his friend had lost his life.

Still Wang Mang did not hurry. He gathered a few papers, went slowly toward the garden, and climbed to the top of the tower which stood on a small island in the middle of an artificial lake joined to the garden by a bridge. There he sat down on a stone seat at a stone table and spread his papers before him. He loved the spot for it looked down into the courts and the garden. His mind began to review his situation. He had a mandate from Heaven and he had tried to carry it out. He had established the New Dynasty in the year 9 and now it was the year 23. He had worked hard and kept nothing for himself. He had revived the writings of the Great Teacher. In fact, he had improved upon them. What more could he have done?

He heard roaring voices in the palace halls. He heard running steps and screams and outcries. No one in the palace had seen him come to the tower for they were used to his lonely ways. He waited.

And then he heard them coming. He looked down and saw them cross the bridge and enter the tower below him. They started up the steps. He sat perfectly still. In that short moment some of the ancient writings came to his mind and he whispered them to himself. Those words would make his enemies powerless he knew.

Suddenly they were there. He saw the flash of a great sword, and that was all. A peasant shouted aloud to all the rest that the usurper was gone.

For two hundred years Wang Mang's skull was kept in the imperial treasury. Was it because he had been a great man, a great emperor, a great usurper? Or was it perhaps because he had dared to be original and history so often honors those who dare to think in their own ways, when it is too late for them to ever know it?

4

Hsuan Tsung

THE EMPEROR WHO LOVED THE ARTS

During the rule of Emperor Hsuan Tsung of the T'ang Dynasty, China came to be known all over the world for her military conquests, her expanding trade, the new ideas which she invited through her foreign contacts, and especially for her development of the fine arts.

Hsuan Tsung, who was also called Ming Huang which means "Brilliant Emperor," began his reign in A.D. 712 when he was only twenty-six. By this time he had developed a circle of friends who had the same tastes as he had. He could easily have spent all of his time in enjoying poetry, in looking at the work of artists, or in listening to music of which he was very fond, but he did not let himself do this.

Instead, he first took on the responsibilities of the ruler of a great empire and did whatever he could to make it even greater. He managed to conquer one of the strongest enemies that was threatening China's northwest. It had Turkish connections, for Central Asia confronted China at this time as it never had before. Hsuan Tsung also succeeded in making an alliance with two other groups to the northwest so that they served to control Mongolia and Turkestan, a clever pact which helped all parties. The Tibetans, too, caused trouble by trying to break free from China but Hsuan Tsung arranged a truce with them. A small nation still further west now appealed to him for help against threatening Arabs. Hsuan Tsung did not send his armies but used diplomacy and succeeded in satisfying the princes who had asked his assistance.

It seemed that he would never get done straightening out his northern neighbors, both those to the northwest and those to the northeast. States in the rugged mountain territory just north of India came asking his help because Tibetan and Arab peoples had formed an alliance against them. What should he do? Hsuan Tsung remembered one of his generals who seemed unusually able. This man, Kao Hsien-chih, came from the Korean peninsula and he had shown his ability as head of the military outposts along China's western borders. He was also vice-governor of Kucha, a city already long famous as a center of music and the arts in what is now Sinkiang Province.

In 747, or perhaps a little earlier than that, Emperor Hsuan Tsung sent for Kao Hsien-chih. When he appeared before him, he seemed to warrant all that the Emperor was going to ask of him. He stood tall, fair-skinned, and brave-looking. He had the bearing of a military man and, while he was courteous, he did not pretend to be humble.

"I want to send you against the alliance of the Arabs and the Tibetans," Hsuan Tsung said, watching his face. "You do not need anyone to point out the difficulties of the undertaking. Not only is there a bitter and cruel enemy to be met, there are those mountains of the Upper Oxus River to be crossed when you start out from Kashgar against the enemy."

The man gave no sign of hesitation. "It is territory I am familiar with. My men are hardened to cold and to rugged mountains," he said.

He was a curious fellow, the Emperor knew, a mixture of warrior, diplomat, and lover of the arts. "What route will you take?" he asked, coming back to the reality of the expedition.

"Through the pass at Kilik or that of Baroghil," Kao answered.

"Both terribly dangerous," the Emperor murmured. The other man did not seem to hear. "But you would have the city of Gilgit as your objective, I suppose," he went on more loudly.

"Gilgit stands on the Indus River," Kao answered simply. It was not necessary to give other reasons for choosing it.

"And, as I suggested, you will set out from Kashgar?"

"From Kashgar."

Emperor Hsuan Tsung asked no further questions. He knew what Kashgar was like for it had been a starting point for many of the invasions against China and one of China's most famous warriors lay buried there. It stood in a fertile spot in China's west, fed by water from the mountain snows, and had an interesting, rich history. Those who passed through, whether going eastward or westward, thought of it as a goal.

Months went by, and then at last, word of the expedition came. It had been successful. News of it gradually spread for it was a remarkable feat. Kao Hsien-chih enjoyed the fame that came to him and reveled in his authority as a military man as well as in his office of governor of a renowned city. His ambitions began to mount. What might he not accomplish in the future? Already China was mistress of most of what is now Afghanistan. She held the key position in Asia and even the Arab peoples had to ask her help. Kao Hsien-chih soon began to act as the Chinese viceroy, or the Emperor's deputy, of all Central Asia. China's fame spread far beyond Central Asia. Persia heard of the expedition and sent ambassadors to the capital at Ch'ang-an with gifts of woolen embroideries, a bed made of agate, and many groups of dancers. Word of China's accomplishments spread throughout the Arab world.

In the East, India and China exchanged ideas of Buddhism and all the arts that were by now connected with it—sculpture, painting, and literature. About a century before Hsuan Tsung's time a Chinese pilgrim had traveled to India overland, to find out more about its religion, and others had followed him. Japan sent a stream of emissaries to the Chinese court to absorb its culture. At home she planned her own capital, Nara, after the Chinese capital. Her whole civilization was patterned after that of her great neighbor. Korea, too, adopted Chinese writing and Chinese ideas. Further south, what was then Indo-China acknowledged Chinese culture as its model.

China learned from those outside her own country, too, for during Hsuan Tsung's reign people of many kinds, with many different purposes, reached China. Buddhism had developed long before in the first century, but now the interchange with India enriched it. Christianity had reached China sometime during the dynasty coming from the Nestorian Christian group in Central Asia, and probably also in India. Arab traders in ports along China's southern coast had brought their Muslim religion with them. There were also a few Jewish traders.

Emperor Hsuan Tsung's capital, Ch'ang-an, was a gay and colorful place. It was the great destination of travelers and traders who had come by the long overland routes from the west. They had dreamed of the city because of all they had heard. Some saw that it was even more than they had expected. They found beautiful Buddhist temples. They found schools based on the old Confucian system of education. They found scholars studying a new form of philosophy called Taoism, based on the teachings of the Lao-tze whom the young Confucius had hoped to see and perhaps had seen. They found a school devoted only to brush writing, or calligraphy, as an art. They found schools of medicine. They found a new institution which the Emperor had started, the Hanlin Academy, which then taught everything from juggling to literature but which would come down in history as the center of serious literary education. Any visitor soon discovered that Hsuan Tsung's court centered around the fine arts of poetry, painting, and music. Poets were his special favorites.

Two of these poets were Li Po and Tu Fu. They wrote in delightfully fresh ways. Chinese poetry often seemed to depend a great deal on illusions to something outside itself, which made it hard for the ordinary reader to understand. While all poetry has some of this suggestive quality, Li Po and Tu Fu wrote more simply than most Chinese poets and charmed the circle of those who gathered around them at the court. Li Po especially liked nature poetry.

As court poets both of these men saw what was going on in the capital and described it in their work. They liked to write about a beautiful woman whom the Emperor took as a secondary wife. She was witty and charming and she became one of China's most famous personalities. Li Po wrote of her as "Flying Swallow."

Emperor Hsuan Tsung was delighted with some of the painters who came to his court. One that he particularly liked was named Wu Tao-tzu, who some authorities say was the greatest of all Chinese painters. Like the poets we have mentioned, he liked to paint landscapes. He put them on the walls of temples in Hsuan Tsung's capital and on walls in the earlier capital, Loyang. He painted so realistically that a story about him says that one day when he and the Emperor were standing looking at a scene on a wall the artist had decorated, Wu Tao-tzu clapped his hands and a door in the scene opened. He walked through it and disappeared as it closed behind him, never to be seen again. However much of a fairy tale that may be, the painting of this artist is still gazed at in delight and wonder today.

Wu Tao-tzu had a friend named Wang Wei who was also a

painter. He liked best to use only Chinese black ink applying it in different intensities or shades, called monochrome art. His landscapes are vigorous, with strong contrasts of bold and delicate strokes, quite unlike the fine, poetic touch of Wu Tao-tzu.

With men like these, life at the Chinese court was more gay and free than it had ever been before. The poets and the artists had a great deal to do with it. The atmosphere is portrayed well in small earthenware sculptures or figurines which catch the liveliness and grace of the times. We can see some of these in American museums. There are mounted horsemen, crouching animals, men and women in court dress, or dancing girls. Polo became a popular court game during this time and so we find among the other images, splendid models of polo players leaning perilously from their mounts. These old figurines look as if they had been worn smooth by time or by many hands that held them lovingly. One can easily imagine why one might have liked to hold them for they are charming, full of life, and sometimes full of humor. The truth is, however, that they were probably grave sculptures buried with a lord or his lady.

Poetry, painting, sculpture, and polo playing were popular activities at the capital and in the court, but at the same time an important step in making books was going on. By now paper and ink, which we call India ink, were plentiful but books still had to be copied by hand. Although the exact date is not known, probably printing started at the beginning of the century when Hsuan Tsung began his reign. It is likely that it was first in the form of seals cut from bone or wood which were pressed into ink and then used to stamp out Buddhist prayers, or someone's name. But a method for reproducing an original had been developed. From there on progress led to the making of block prints to reproduce both words and pictures.

As the years went by, Emperor Hsuan Tsung was so in love with the arts that it was more and more difficult for him to give his great empire the attention it should have. He would like to think only of his poetry circle, his schools, his artists and his own religious theories of Taoism. He loved the court ceremonies and had them performed with great magnificence, but he paid less and less attention to the business of the court.

Another influence that made him less interested in affairs of state than he should have continued to be was his secondary wife, Yang Kuei-fei, about whom Li Po wrote. She loved a gay life and encouraged the Emperor in it, too. Gradually power started to slip from his hands. A rebellion sprang up led by a man who had non-Chinese blood in his veins and who was a military leader. He had demonstrated what he could do in some battles against tribes in the north and the Emperor and his beautiful wife had come to trust him. They let him hold an important military position in the government never doubting his loyalty. But in A.D. 755 he openly started a revolt and seized territory just north of the Yellow River.

When news of the revolt reached the Emperor he knew that Ch'ang-an was in danger—it would be the rebel's next objective. The Emperor tried to escape with Yang Kuei-fei and some of her relatives who had been given positions in the government. As they were making their escape, rations for the soldier guards ran out. They mutinied and killed one of Yang Kuei-fei's cousins who was with them, put his head on the point of a lance and brought it defiantly to the Emperor. As an added threat, they killed two of Yang Kuei-fei's sisters in the same way and presented their heads. Hsuan Tsung was thoroughly terrified. He went to the soldiers and tried to reason with them. Instead, they now demanded the life of his beloved wife and he was not able to save her. After these executions they seemed to be satisfied for they re-formed their ranks and continued their escape. What did anything matter now? The Emperor was carried on toward Szechuan Province, the destination of the flight.

While Hsuan Tsung was continuing his flight, the usurper occupied the capital. It was the year A.D. 756, the end of a great and shining period of Chinese history, but history would never let it be forgotten. Poetry and painting, music and sculpture, trade contacts with the western world, cultural exchange, the deepening of Confucian scholarship rooted in the new Hanlin Academy, the beginning of printing—all were signs of a magnificent age during which the greatest emperor of the T'ang Dynasty ruled China. The T'ang Dynasty would always be referred to as one of China's great, if not her greatest, period. Always, too, Hsuan Tsung would be recalled as the Brilliant Emperor while Yang Kuei-fei would be immortalized in art and poetry and drama through the ages to come.

5

1021–1086

Wang An-shih

PRACTICAL POLITICIAN

If anyone is in need of money for a wedding or a funeral,
  I will lend it to him to dispel his anxiety.
If anyone has had a poor harvest,
  I will give him all the grain that I possess so that he
    has something to live on.
If the crops are plentiful, I collect them:
If they are insufficient, I give out all that I possess
  so that work may go on.
In these days people bother little about them, but for my
  part I am resolved to put down the speculators.

This is a poem by a down-to-earth reformer, a minister in the Chinese court in the eleventh century, a time when China was trying to repel invasions by the Mongols. He saw that the country was in danger and he had ideas of how to save her. Although he did not have much use for fine-sounding theories, he knew how to use words for he came from a scholarly background, respected Confucian literature, and had many new ideas about education. But he was poor and he understood the problems of the poor.

As a boy Wang An-shih worked hard at school. People said that when he was writing a composition his brush pen flew over the paper. When he grew to be a man he refused to pay any attention to things that would mark him as an educated person, a gentleman. He did not care how he looked and often forgot to wash his face or have his hair combed. He did not change his clothes as frequently as he should and presented a generally disheveled appearance. His mind was on other things for when he was still quite a young man he began to have strange, new, strong ideas about what was wrong with the Chinese government and its officials. And yet, in spite of his serious thoughts about his country, Wang An-shih loved poetry, and whenever he could, he wrote it for his own pleasure.

As he grew older he concentrated on the problems of government and corrupt officials and decided to throw his energies into doing something about them. He wanted to strengthen the government and improve the living conditions of ordinary people—two things which he believed depended on each other. He felt that he ought not to place pressure on the emperor to make reforms without first undertaking a thorough study of the whole situation. In order to do this he set out on long journeys through the west, the south, and to the capital which was at this time in Kai-feng. His home was in the Yangtze Valley so he already knew that part of the country. Wherever he went, he found three things to be true. Officials were dishonest, and cared only for themselves. The common people had no one to champion them. The country was without strong military defenses.

When Wang An-shih returned from his travels he started sending messages, or memorials, to Emperor Sheng-tsung. In a document in which Wang An-shih outlined his whole basic plan, called *Ten Thousand Word Memorial,* he said that the Emperor was wise, reverent, frugal, and hard-working. He pointed out that the Emperor was not interested in music, beautiful women, dogs, horses, or sight-seeing. He said that the ruler had feeling for the common people. All in all, Wang An-shih said that with such a good ruler the empire should be in good shape, but that was not at all the case; quite the contrary was true. The trouble, he said, was that the nation was facing new problems that had to be met in new ways. While these might be based on the ancient principles, methods had to be altered to meet the times.

The Emperor found the wording of this first long memorial polite, almost gentle. But as another, yet another, and then a stream of them came, he saw that this hot-headed young reformer had no intention of small, gentle changes in the ways things were being done. He wanted to pull problems up and examine their roots. Of course, it was true that the national budget was always in the red, and getting more so. It was true that the Mongols were more and more threatening. Perhaps Wang An-shih's ideas had something to recommend them the Emperor decided and sent for the man.

Wang An-shih stood before the Emperor with no signs of uneasiness or awe. He looked slouchily comfortable, as though he might have just gotten out of bed. The Emperor thought momentarily of sending him home to make himself more presentable for an audience, and then put the idea out of mind. It was really not important. He had heard a great deal about this man and everything indicated that he was really devoted to his country.

"I have read your memorials," Sheng-tsung, the Emperor, began.

"They are not worthy of imperial attention," Wang answered, remembering Confucian rules of courtesy toward one's sovereign though he *was* young.

"Your proposals are worthy of serious thought," the Emperor continued. "Our country has many problems and one of the greatest is its economy, as you have pointed out."

"Then it should be reorganized from the rice-stubble up," Wang said, but remembered to drop his head to show respect even though his words came abruptly.

"Where would you suggest beginning?"

"Wherever the landlords are forming monopolies, oppressing the small merchants and businesses, evading the taxes."

"And where do you say these places are?"

"In my province, Kiangsi, in Szechuan, in Kwangtung," Wang answered quickly. "I have been to these places to see for myself, and I know the conditions."

"I have asked you to come here for two reasons," the Emperor said carefully, looking at him hard. "You have mentioned them both. You have cared enough to make a survey. You come from Kiangsi and, as you must know, there are important Kiangsi people at court who will support your proposals if only because they want to overpower the group from the province of Szechuan." The Emperor watched Wang's face while he was speaking.

"I have no interest at all in cliques," Wang said, throwing his head back proudly. "I'm only interested in restoring the glory of China as the Middle Kingdom, and in the welfare of the common people. These two causes cannot be separated from each other."

What a man this was, the Emperor thought. He wished that he had as much self-assurance, the same free spirit. Well, then, he would let the fellow test his ideas and show what he could do.

"Since what has been tried so far has failed, since the enemy from the northwest presses us harder and harder and since the economy becomes weaker day by day, I will appoint you a minister at the court and give you an opportunity to prove your theories," he said.

Wang An-shih bowed low, clasped his hands together and shook them in a gesture of greeting and farewell, and started backing away, careful not to turn his back on the sovereign.

When he was disappearing between the guards, the Emperor's voice rang out suddenly, bringing him to a quick halt. He stepped forward and waited.

"You write memorials with grace, and I have heard that you also write poetry. Quote a verse for me so that I will not always think of my duties." The young ruler's voice was almost pleading.

Wang An-shih's eyes shone and he seemed suddenly an altogether different person from the reformer he had been a few minutes earlier. He stepped closer to the Emperor. A guard stepped with him. He began to quote, his gaze fixed on some distant point.

> *The incense stick is burned to ash,*
> *   the water-clock is stilled,*
> *The midnight breeze blows sharply by,*
> *   and all around is stilled.*
>
> *Yet I am kept from slumber*
> *   by the beauty of the spring . . .*
> *Sweet shapes of flowers across the blind*
> *   the quivering moonbeams fling.*

When he had finished, he looked at the Emperor and caught his pleased expression. "You have written it in one of the most difficult meters," he said. "I shall think of it often, though I rarely see the signs of spring of which the poem speaks."

"Sir, yours is a greater opportunity than to write foolish poems about spring, or even than to regret not seeing its signs. You are Emperor of China, Emperor of the greatest country on earth, and one which your humble servant wishes to keep so."

Wang An-shih half wondered whether it could be he who was saying the words he heard, for they were polite and humble, when in reality his head was swelling with pride and his self-assurance was almost choking him. Not only had he been appointed a minister; his poetry had been praised.

"Well said," the Emperor answered, again the sovereign. "Bring me your exact proposals that I may see what they are and how they can be put into practice."

Wang An-shih worked furiously getting his proposals ready to present. He found the other Kiangsi people at court ready to cooperate but he could not trust their motives. Were they just trying to strengthen their own group, or were they really interested in bettering the condition of the whole country? He was not going to pay too much attention to them. His pen brushed hundreds of characters stating his ideas which were devastating to the old ways of doing things. The basis of education Wang An-shih declared must be changed. The civil service examination which a student had to take so as to have any status and any possibility of getting a political appointment should require a familiarity with a wide group of practical subjects instead of only a discussion of literary styles. A later Chinese writer said that Wang An-shih started so revolutionary a trend that even the pupils at village schools threw away their rhetoric textbooks and began to study pioneers of history, geography, and political economy.

Wang An-shih said that reforms ought to be based on the original ideas of Confucius for these had been misinterpreted. He prepared a sample interpretation of his own and sent it along. (As time passed he would do a great deal of this reinterpreting.) He proposed that the government should have complete charge of all commerce, should regulate prices, and should make loans to farmers at reasonable rates of interest. He said that those who were wealthy ought to carry more of the weight of taxes. He stated that military defense was everyone's business and that each family ought to belong to a local militia. His proposals were aimed at changing the three major evils he had found in his survey of the country—corruption of officials, the suffering of the common people, and weakness in the military system.

The Emperor read Wang An-shih's memorials carefully and then told him to put them into practice. Some of the ideas succeeded. At first he won his place at court as a person because of his charm and his self-assurance. He gradually advanced until he was a prime minister. But in spite of the fact that some of his ideals were acclaimed as good ones and in spite of the fact that he was a personal success, he gradually ran into opposition.

As the opposition increased he failed to see that it was both because his measures were too hard on the wealthy and powerful, and because he was too overbearing as he became more important. He was now so determined to bring about success for his ideas that when anyone did not agree with him, he grew unpleasantly stubborn. The reforms which were to have been put into effect by the whole state machinery became instead his own private projects because no one could work with him.

One of the older statesmen came to him one day and said, "Do not do things that are against human feeling or you will lose the support of others." When Wang An-shih first looked blank and then angry, the man who had come to him added gently, "It is not that we do not support you in what you want to do; we cannot go along with the way you do it." He saw it was useless to remonstrate with the reformer. He and the other ministers and statesmen who really wanted to help carry out the changes proposed, turned against Wang An-shih more and more. He became a single flaming torch trying to start a great fire of change. He failed to see that the torch was about to be blown out by too much wind of opposition.

A historian named Ssu-ma Kuang was one of Wang An-shih's strongest opponents. As a conservative he naturally was against all the new laws that the Emperor began putting into effect as soon as Wang An-shih came to court in A.D. 1069. Therefore, he resigned in protest and began to write a great chronological history of China which he called *General Mirror*. He did not return to court until the Emperor died in A.D. 1085 but then became a prime minister, a position which Wang An-shih had held for many years. Ssu-ma Kuang turned on him and abolished many of the reforms that were still in effect. The historian addressed the new Emperor, a boy who was only fifteen years old, praising the former Emperor and blaming Wang An-shih for failing to have any human feelings and for being self-satisfied and opinionated. When Wang An-shih heard of what he had said he replied by saying that the scholars, or the conservatives, were only willing to walk in the footsteps of their ancestors instead of being willing to test new roads and new directions.

From this exchange on it was a back and forth game between reformist and conservative. The argument was going to go on even after Wang An-shih died, a year after Ssu-ma Kuang returned to court. And yet history was to show that Wang An-shih had done something worthwhile for his country because he had made her leaders stop and think and evaluate what they were doing. He had revolutionized education by spreading a fresh interpretation of classical literature and by establishing free education and building many schools. His vigorous defense of the original Chinese philosophical ideas weakened Buddhism which had been growing strong since the previous T'ang Dynasty, and turned scholars back to their own sources.

Wang An-shih had wanted to save China from the northern peoples who were growing so strong, by making her undefeatable from within. His proposals of how to do this helped, but the careful diplomacy which the court practiced also helped. In spite of these good efforts, disaster could not be held off indefinitely. In A.D. 1125 the Mongols marched against the

Sung capital more powerfully than ever before and captured it. They also took the Emperor and his aged father. What historians called the Northern Sung Dynasty had come to an end. The Chinese fled southward and made Nanking their capital a year later.

By this time Wang An-shih had been dead forty years. The controversies he had stirred up were dead—or were they? His ideas would be discussed down through the centuries. He would be linked with Wang Mang, the earlier socialist emperor, and later with Dr. Sun Yat-sen the leader of the modern Chinese revolution. He would even be linked with the Chinese People's Republic, because he believed that a state had to be responsible for the welfare of its people.

6

Hung Hsiu-Ch'uan

LEADER OF THE TAIPING REBELLION

Hung Hsiu-Ch'uan, a strange, magnetic, exciting man who was to have a great influence over Chinese history was born into a South China tribal group which lived near Canton. Even though they were only peasants, his family and his relatives decided that he ought to be educated so they cooperated in sending him to school to prepare for the civil service examinations given yearly in Canton. They hoped that he would be able to get an official government position. When he went to take the examination for the first time, he was quite sure that he would return as a success. Instead, he failed miserably. He tried the next year, and the next. Each time he failed to pass the examination. His trying and failing gradually became almost routine.

On one of these yearly trips to Canton, when he was twenty-two, Hung passed a little church where the doors stood open to the street. He could hear a man speaking inside, and the speech was curious for many of the words were not pronounced correctly. A small crowd had gathered inside. Out of curiosity he entered, picked up some leaflets displayed on a table, and dropped onto one of the benches in the rear. Thor-

oughly discouraged about ever passing the examination, by
this time he was almost ready to give up trying. Yet when he
really faced that thought his heart sank and his whole life plan
seemed to be so hopeless that he could not accept that alterna-
tive either. He started half-heartedly reading the pamphlets he
had picked up but the voice of the man who was speaking
soon arrested his attention. Hung straightened up so as to see
him over the heads of the people in front of him. Then, because some of them were standing, he rose to his feet and took
a few steps forward in order to get a clear view of the speaker.
As he had suspected, he was a foreigner, a pale, anemic-look-
ing person, his short hair thinning, his intense, urgent voice
preaching about One God and a Jesus. He made curious language mistakes, sometimes using the wrong tone for a word so
that it came out with an entirely different meaning from what
he probably intended. Now and again a ripple of laughter
passed over the people who were listening. Yet they were
straining to hear what the man had to say, too.

The foreigner talked about God as a heavenly father, and
all men as his sons, and of Jesus as one divinely begotten by
Him and sent to the world to save all others from having to go
to purgatory to be punished for their sins. He talked about a
Kingdom of Heaven. Hung like the way he described it.

Hung listened until the meeting was over, then he disappeared into the crowd. He folded the leaflets and put them in
an inside pocket. He planned to read them carefully sometime.
He would have liked to have asked a little more about this
Jesus Club the preacher kept referring to, for that was the way
he translated "Christian Church." Perhaps if he stayed and
talked to the Chinese man who was sitting up in front in
charge of the meeting he might find out a good deal more. But
no, that man was probably paid to say the right thing. He
would wait and ask other people who could speak freely about
all this.

What Hung had to do first, in any case, was to pass that civil service examination. All of his life had so far been aimed at that one objective. Yet he failed and failed. Next year he would not fail!

During the coming months he worked harder than ever before. He grew thin because he could not sleep and because he lost his appetite. But he had made up his mind to succeed, now, and nothing else mattered. The days, weeks, and months passed, and the time of the examination arrived.

Pale and thin, but determined, Hung set out for Canton and the examination halls where hundreds of students would do nothing but write long discourses on their interpretations of Confucian ideas and historic points of view. Poetry, philosophy, economic theories—all were part of the wide-scoped field of knowledge they were supposed to have mastered. Most important was the ability to be able to express oneself clearly, yet gracefully, in the scholarly written Chinese form, *wen-li*, which resembles Chaucerian English.

Hung reached the examination hall and settled to his work. The topics to be written about this year were dreadful. He felt his mind go blank. Everything was suddenly far away, out of reach. He struggled to master himself, and poured and drank cup after cup of tea from the teapot that was furnished. At last he began to write slowly with a hand that he could barely hold steady. Each day was worse than the one before because he was losing confidence in himself. He felt himself failing, almost slipping into some abyss, barely keeping out of it by clinging desperately to its crumbling edges. At last his hold gave out and he tumbled into bottomless darkness.

After months of being very ill at home, he saw a light. He did not know that it was a dream. He had three strange dreams. In the first he saw an old man who complained that instead of worshiping him, people were worshiping demons. In the second, Confucius appeared. A voice was scolding him and telling him to repent. Confucius repent? It was unbelievable. Yet that was what Hung saw. In a third dream a middle-aged man came and told Hung how to destroy demons. When the dreams were over Hung kept thinking about them. He tried to decide what they meant. Of course! He had it! The old man was the foreign preacher's God the Heavenly Father, much like the old Chinese idea of the Supreme Being or Heaven. Jesus was the middle-aged man, or Elder Brother, and he was telling him, Hung, the Younger Brother, to stamp out demon-worship. Hung thought of all worship of images as demon-worship and the country was full of Buddhist temples with their idols.

When he was well, Hung became a teacher in the village school. One day he remembered the leaflets he had picked up in the church in Canton, having kept them carefully all this time, and began to study them. They told about the Bible and what it taught. He decided he had to know more about Christianity so he went to Canton and looked for someone who could teach him. He found a missionary who held very conservative ideas, and stayed with him for two months. What he learned gave him the impression that the religion was supernatural, almost magical. The ideas he already had about being told what he must do in those visions or dreams now became strong and clear. Although the missionary may not have known what plans were developing in his pupil's mind, Hung saw a kingdom ruled by himself, a Kingdom of Heaven, with him at the head.

Back home among his relatives Hung began to talk about his dreams and about the orders he had been given. He said that his study in Canton had made his mandate from Heaven even clearer. He was so convincing in his self-assurance that his own people listened to him and believed him. They held a conference and agreed that their first step was certainly to go and break up idols everywhere for these stood for demon-worship. They went out in a band and destroyed images first in one village and then in another. The people in these places could scarcely believe what they saw. This Hung family was taking away their only hope of help in bad times and wasting the money which had been collected with such difficulty to make and repair the idols. The villagers gathered and shouted out their anger. They threw stones and beat the intruders with sticks.

"Go! Leave this place and never come again!" they shouted. "We will report what you have done to the magistrate."

Hung gave up his schoolteaching and, at the head of members of his own clan, he went to the next province to get others from his tribe to join them. The people came quickly because they were intrigued by his certainty of what he was to do and pleased with being called God-Worshipers. Wherever they went in that province they had some trouble with the authorities, but it was not enough to discourage Hung.

Many conditions throughout China in the middle of the nineteenth century helped his group to grow at an amazing speed. In the last part of the 1840's China had severe famines. The British had defeated China in what is called the Opium War, a war fought to force China to trade with the West, and had obtained rights to open ports to this trade by means of treaties. The government in Peking was under the Manchus rather than Chinese rulers, and the Chinese felt that the Manchus, too, were foreigners of whom they should be freed. A spirit of revolt was strong everywhere.

Revolt could break out most easily where government control was weakest. The southern province where Hung and his followers were active was such a spot. While there were other dangerous rebel groups in the country, Hung's was particularly strong because of his own conviction about what he was called to do and because he had an organization. The more officials troubled him, the more determined he became to start a great revolt against the government which now symbolized the enemy, or the demon-worshipers, simply because it opposed his God-Worshipers. The rebel group improved its organization. It formed an army. It set up a common treasury where funds from personal property that was now sold were pooled. It began to make weapons. It indoctrinated everyone who joined it.

This indoctrination was important. It began with a firmly carried out discipline. The leaders sincerely believed in their cause and displayed a bravery that impressed their followers. Devotion to the cause was strong partly because Hung made it clear that no earthly rewards were to be expected; the only reward was a spiritual one and came in the afterlife. Although the people who first joined him and his family were a curious lot of misfits and vagabonds who had nothing to lose, the purpose of the rebellion—to overthrow the government—soon attracted others.

In December, 1850, the rebels met a full-scale attack by government forces, and won. Hung was triumphant. He proclaimed himself Heavenly King and his regime the Heavenly Kingdom of Great Peace. Great Peace is *tai ping* in Chinese, so history calls Hung's movement the Taiping Rebellion.

The first great success attracted thousands of new followers. Many of these were respectable citizens who wanted a change of government. After all, it seemed as though Hung had answers to many of China's problems. The worship of one god instead of many was acceptable because it would unify the country and because there was a precedent for it in ancient worship of Heaven carried out formally every year by emperors in Peking. The people supported the rebellion both in order to change the government and to get rid of the foreigners who kept biting off more and more of their country through wars and treaties. The fact that the God-Worshipers had a common treasury, that they considered everyone as brothers and sisters whatever their social background, appealed especially to the poor. They rushed to affiliate themselves with the Great Peace movement.

The rebels were now determined to conquer China for themselves. They moved northward to the Yangtze River Valley, aiming at Nanking. In order to avoid strong opposition they stayed away from big towns and cities on the way. In 1853 they occupied the city and renamed it Heavenly Capital, a suitable thing to do since they were still sure that they were establishing a Heavenly Kingdom under divine orders. The chief military commander often claimed that God told him what strategic moves to make.

With Nanking in their hands, the rebels sent forces northward toward Peking and then also westward. Sometimes the leaders of these expeditions were successful, but more often they were defeated. In the meantime, the capital was having to carry on a constant battle with the people in the heavily populated river valley. This state of things went on for ten years, ruining the richest part of China.

At the same time, two great leaders, government officials Tseng Kuo-fan and Li Hung-chang, were strongly opposing the rebellion. They reorganized and improved the government forces wherever the rebels were advancing so that the resistance to them was strong.

A curious thing about Hung was that he never seemed to wonder what Western Christian people thought of what he was doing. He had taken over many Christian ideas, if in a mixed-up fashion. He even had ten commandments a great deal like those in the Old Testament. One of the poems he used for his teachings went like this:

> *Jesus was a crown Prince,*
> *Whom God sent to earth in ancient times.*
> *He sacrificed his life for the sins of men,*
> *Being the first to offer meritorious service.*

It was hard to bear the Cross:
Grieving clouds darkened the sun.
The noble Prince from Heaven,
Died for you—men and women . . .

Another says:

Whether to be noble or mean is for you to choose.
To be a real man you must make an effort to improve yourself.
Follow the teaching of the Ten Commandments:
You will enjoy the blessings of Paradise.

For a while missionaries from Europe and America believed that the Taiping Rebellion might be a fine thing. Perhaps Christianity had at last taken root in China. The organization's discipline was good and its economic program seemed to be realistic. A statement published in 1853 showed what Hung Hsiu-ch'uan intended to do about the ownership of land. All land was to be distributed to families on the basis of the number of persons in a family. It was to be divided also on the basis of its fertility so that each family would have both good and bad land and none would be favored or discriminated against. All harvests were to be supervised by the government so that surpluses could be stored. Harvests were to be shared across the country so no areas would go hungry while others had more than they needed. Villagers were to plant mulberry trees to feed silkworms around their villages and all the women were to raise the worms, spin the silk, and weave it into cloth.

Hung believed that he was reestablishing the Chinese imperial line to replace the Manchu foreigners now on the throne. He made his men followers stop braiding their hair in queues as the Manchus had ordered them to do as a sign of their servitude to the invader-rulers. Hung had them knot it on top of their heads again in the original Chinese fashion for, of course, short hair was a Western idea taken over much later.

Watching what was going on, the Western foreigners may have thought that if the Taipings succeeded in overthrowing the Manchu dynasty, they would be much easier to deal with than the present rulers. But they soon saw that the rebel leaders were fanatics. They still believed that they were chosen and that they could not do anything wrong. When the Taipings began to threaten the city of Shanghai, which was China's most important center of trade with the outside world, the Westerners became alarmed.

They would not have needed to be afraid for the city, for while the Yangtze Valley was being ruined by the rebellion, Hung himself was losing control. He gradually stopped being a leader and just relaxed in Nanking, relying on the belief that as a holy emperor he could not do anything wrong even though he was by now breaking his own disciplines. When he found that the man who had shared responsibility for leading the rebellion with him more than anyone else was dreaming of taking the throne in Nanking from him, Hung started a bloody purge which took that man's life along with those of many others. He replaced men he had formerly trusted with members of his own family.

A general named Li who was still loyal to Hung at last became so alarmed about the way things were going that he came to Nanking to warn his master. He found Hung still sure that he had been called to lead his cause and still sure that nothing was going to happen to him. Li tried to make him more realistic.

"Don't you see that your forces are being pushed back more and more and are now clustered around Nanking? Don't you see that they are being defeated?"

"Who can defeat the Taipings?" Hung asked proudly.

"Tseng Kuo-fan can," Li answered sharply. "He is not for the Manchus but he is for a national government."

"If he is not for the Heavenly Kingdom then he is against any national government," Hung retorted. "None can conquer the Heavenly Kingdom or the Heavenly King." His eyes were fixed on nothing, his voice vague.

"I tell you Tseng's forces are strong and he has a good helper in the person of Li Hung-chang. They are going to march on this city."

Hung did not answer.

"You have heard of a man named Gordon, the English soldier, one of those who have been troubling the Empress Dowager, forcing the Treaty of Tientsin? [Result of the wars between Great Britain and China in 1856-1860 following the Opium Wars.] Well, he has come to Shanghai now."

"I have heard that the Europeans are so afraid of the armies of the Heavenly Kingdom that they are gathering troops in Shanghai," Hung said. "For a while they had an American man named Ward in charge of them but now he is dead." His expression of self-assurance did not change.

"Yes, he was killed in the fighting but he made Shanghai secure from our forces, and now they have put the man Gordon in his place."

"The Americans in the foreign army will never follow a Britisher," Hung said cannily.

"But they *are* following him," Li answered. "I hear that he knows the country well. He has studied how the canals run, where the most strongly walled cities are. He knows which roads are good enough for his guns to be moved along them."

"No power can defeat the Taipings," Hung repeated, falling back into a dull monotone. "They believe in a God who leads them and in their Heavenly Emperor."

"I am told that Gordon's men believe just as much in him. They say that he can send them into battle armed with only a cane, and they are victors because of their spirit! Such is his power to make them believe in their cause!"

"It will fail," Hung said doggedly.

This conversation took place in March, 1863. By November of that year the great walled city, Soochow, fell to the armies of Charles George Gordon. When Li had the news he hurried to Nanking again and stood before the Heavenly Emperor.

"That foreign Gordon has captured Soochow, but now he says he is not going to fight any more because the Chinese generals under him beheaded your rebel leaders when he had promised that they would be treated with clemency if they surrendered." Even while Li reported this he could scarcely believe it himself.

"It cannot be true," Hung said, interested in spite of himself. "What general would not behead enemy leaders defeated in battle? Who would pay any attention to promises—much less make them in the first place? This shows that Gordon is a fool and can never defeat the Heavenly Army."

"But he *has* taken Soochow," Li insisted.

"You said he is not going to fight any more," Hung answered.

"When he understands the Chinese customs in war, he will come back," Li said. "You will see."

He was right. After six months during which Gordon withdrew his men and refused to have any part in suppressing the Taipings, he came back. He felt that he must do all he could to bring peace to the rich valley that was being ruined by the constant fighting.

In May, 1864, his troops and those in the imperial army took the main Taiping military stronghold. Word of it came to Nanking. When Hung heard the news he paid no attention to it for he still believed that he could never be defeated. Then Li, his friend, came again quickly.

"Escape! Escape while there is still time," he begged.

"There is no need for the Heavenly Emperor to escape," Hung said, pulling his imperial yellow robes more closely around him and pushing his hands up into his long sleeves. "Gordon has withdrawn his troops again," he added, "so do not talk to me about his ability."

"He does not need to stay with the imperial forces any longer for he has already taken our greatest stronghold in the Yangtze Valley. Now Tseng Kuo-fan is leading the march on Nanking." Li was surprised that Hung knew that Gordon had quit the fighting, but it did not make any difference now. The capital was doomed. "Aren't you going to leave?" he asked again.

"Leave? I, the Heavenly Emperor chosen by God, leave the capital of the Heavenly Kingdom?"

Li went away. He was still loyal to his friend and now he was heartbroken for him. He felt sure that this man whom he, too, had believed was chosen to save his people, was going to be killed.

A few days after his visit when the imperial troops captured Nanking, they looked for the Heavenly Emperor. For a long time they could not find him anywhere. Then, at last, someone shouted from the sewers under the palace. Others rushed down. There he lay, wrapped in his soiled yellow robes, dead. He had taken poison.

When Li heard what had happened, he felt sad but he knew that this man's life was not going to be wasted even though his cause had failed. Others still to come would remember Hung who had led the Taipings and would say that he was the fore-runner of change, the torchbearer for a new China. Some would insist that he was only a madman, but others would believe that he truly had a vision, even if a strange one and hard for others to understand.

Li's prediction was true. Within the next half-century new

Chinese leaders would think of the Taiping Rebellion when they started China's modern Nationalist Revolution. They would acknowledge that this most strange of several rebellions of different sorts that took place during the Manchu dynasty, had strongly influenced their own dreams of a new China. They were, in a way, followers of the whirlwind leader of the Taiping Rebellion.

7

1834–1908

The Empress Dowager

Tzu Hsi

CHINA'S GREATEST WOMAN RULER

In the middle of the nineteenth century, China was under great pressure to change from an ancient nation into a modern one. The pressure came from two directions. From the outside, foreign powers demanded that her Manchu rulers recognize the representatives they sent to the Dragon Throne in Peking and allow them to stay in the capital. On the inside, young Chinese were getting new ideas from the teaching of Christian missionaries. They were learning the English language so that they were able to read more and more about the Western world. They demanded that China modernize, if not by revolution then at least by rapid reforms.

Of course, there had already been reformers like Wang Mang and Wang An-shih but they had not succeeded in basically changing their government. The Taiping Rebellion was still going on in the Yangtze River Valley but it was turning out to be only a fanatical uprising that had to be put down.

The one person in Peking who was most opposed to change at this time was a powerful young woman who was a secondary wife to the reigning Manchu emperor, Hsien Feng. Her name was Yehonala and she came from an important Manchu family. She was very beautiful, very clever, fearless, and highly ambitious. She had been educated at home so that she could read both the ordinary Chinese characters and the classical literary language *wen-li*. Since she was only a little girl she had known Jung Lu, a distant relative, who often came to her home. When they grew up they fell in love with each other and Jung Lu asked her to marry him. This was possible because Manchus did not follow the Chinese custom of parents arranging marriage for their children. Yehonala hesitated. During that short hesitation a royal summons came from the court asking her to present herself there. Many carefully selected girls would be asked to go. It was not easy to refuse such a summons for it was considered a great honor to be included among the girls from whom the Emperor would choose his first wife, or consort, and some secondary wives. One of Yehonala's cousins was being asked to go, too.

Yehonala decided to present herself to the Emperor. Jung Lu was already a guardsman at the gates of the Forbidden City, the innermost part of the palace grounds. If she were chosen she might still see him sometimes at the palace.

The exciting moment came. Hundreds of girls walked slowly before the Emperor and his mother so that he could make his choice. He chose Yehonala's cousin to be his consort for he had once loved her older sister and she had died. Then he chose Yehonala as the first of his secondary wives. She stood out among the other girls because of her beauty and her spirit. Something about her attracted his attention almost at once.

When Yehonala found that Emperor Hsien Feng was a weak and dissipated man, she could scarcely endure him. Her heart flew to Jung Lu. She wondered how she could ever have given him up for the wretched sovereign. Yet, she was ambitious. If she could learn to control the Emperor's decisions, she might become very powerful herself. If he should die young, she might become the regent because . . . his mother was already old and ill. If she bore him a son. . . . Her dreams sprang up and began to leap ahead. But all that was far away. During those first weeks in the palace she thought of Jung Lu again and again. She was very lonely and she was like a prisoner in the beautiful courts that were hers.

At last Yehonala found a way to bribe one of the palace servants to summon Jung Lu for a secret meeting. They heartbrokenly pledged their love to each other forever, even though they would always have to hide it.

Now Yehonala put her mind on how she could prepare herself for greater power, how she might be able to make her dreams come true. Every day she had many hours of free time to spend because everything was done for her and she could not leave her own section of the palace grounds. She decided to study and become acquainted with the history and geography of China and to learn her classics better. She asked for an instructor and for a place where she might read and keep her books. An old man was assigned to teach her and a small library was prepared for her. As she spent hours there with him she became more and more proud of China, which she thought of as her country even though she was a Manchu. It was right to keep foreign influences out. No foreign power ought ever to be recognized, she thought, or to have permission to send representatives to the court, unless they came with tribute as subject nations.

The first step in Yehonala's dreams for herself worked well. She gave birth to a boy. This automatically increased her power because he was heir to the throne. Her cousin, the consort, had only given birth to a girl. Yehonala was determined that no one should ever rob her son of his right and her of her new authority because of him.

When the baby was a month old, the imperial court planned to celebrate his birth according to custom. There were to be feasts all through the empire, too. The Emperor sent a servant to Yehonala to ask her what special kind of celebration she would like best, and she said, a play. She loved plays and she never saw them here in the palace. But the play was only a minor part of the day's program for there was a great procession with all the royal princes and eunuchs and ministers, each dressed in his appropriate regal dress. Hundreds of gifts came from across the country. These were carried in by dozens of servants and presented after the Emperor had taken his place on the golden throne.

Yehonala and her cousin, the consort, had to watch all this ceremony from seats behind a carved screen which stood back of the throne, for women were not allowed to appear publicly before the audience. But they could see everything through the openings of the carving, though others could not see them. When all the gifts had been accepted Yehonala's turn to be honored came. The Emperor summoned her to stand before him and she was led to that place. She sank to her knees, crossed her hands on the tiled floor in front of her and bent her forehead to her hands in a deep obeisance. She waited for the Emperor to speak.

"I do this day decree that the mother of the Imperial Heir, here kneeling, is to be raised to the rank of Consort, equal in all ways to the present Consort. That there be no confusion, the present Consort shall be known as Tzu An, Empress of the Eastern Palace, and the Fortunate Mother shall be known as Tzu Hsi, Empress of the Western Palace. This is my will. It shall be declared across the realm, that it may be known to all people."

Yehonala bowed her head upon her hands three times, then again three times, and another three times before she rose and putting her hand on the arm of the eunuch who had brought her forward, returned to her seat. The great hall was so still that one could hear a deep breath drawn. Her own breath was coming fast and her heart was beating hard. Who could harm her now? Who could limit her? She was mother of the emperor to be, Imperial Consort, and one day, Empress Dowager of the Dragon Throne of China.

The Emperor was often ill. One day when she was called from her own courts to see him, she persuaded him to always let her sit near him behind the screen when he was on the throne holding public audience, so that she could share his burdens of state. "I will listen to what the ministers say, and when they are gone, I will tell you what I think, but I will leave all the decisions to you," she said. The Emperor was so ill and weary that he gradually let her take more and more authority even though he kept it secret.

One day an audience was called especially because of the dangerous situation in the south. The viceroy from Kwangtung Province had hurried to the capital by boat and horseback. Tzu Hsi listened to his report. He said that traders from the West were causing trouble because, they claimed, the Chinese had insulted their flag. They demanded an apology from him as a representative of the Chinese government. He believed that this was all only an excuse to make larger and larger demands. The British in particular wanted better trade privileges so that they and their families could live in Canton. They wanted more rights for their ships on Chinese rivers. The viceroy said if the foreigners were denied what they asked they might make war again as they had only a few years earlier. Another trouble was that the people in the south were protesting against the foreigners in their newspapers which were pasted on public walls for everyone to see. When the foreigners found out what these papers said, they claimed that they were being insulted. But, the viceroy asked, dared he silence the people too severely? There was always the danger of rebellion.

When Tzu Hsi heard what the viceroy was saying, it was all

she could do to be still behind the screen. Yet she knew she must not speak. She must wait until more power was in her hands. *She* would send armies to free China of the foreigners for once and all, if she had *her* way!

The British were not easily put off. They threatened to sail northward to a seaport called Tientsin and attack Taku Forts at the harbor entrance. The Emperor was ill with fear when he received this word. He summoned his brother Prince Kung who was a seasoned statesman. Prince Kung arrived when Tzu Hsi was with the Emperor arguing openly for war against the foreigners.

"Let them return to their own lands," she cried. "We have tried to be patient but still they are troubling us."

"We cannot make them leave," Prince Kung said.

"Then we can kill them and throw them into the sea," Tzu Hsi declared, her eyes blazing. Why were these two brothers so timid! Why did no one dare do anything?

"They would only come back stronger than ever," Prince Kung said sadly. "There is only one way and that is to put them off, to delay even longer."

"Have it your way," Tzu Hsi answered, "but in the end we will have to destroy them." She lifted her head proudly and looked full at first one and then the other of the two men. The Emperor, though he loved her, trembled at her self-assurance. She comforted him because she was never uncertain of what to do. Prince Kung thought uneasily that she had better leave the capital and go to the Summer Palace in the hills outside the city until the summer months were over, for she was too clever and too daring. No telling what plan she might contrive.

When the summer was past, Prince Kung came to Peking again because he was so worried about the foreigners in the south. He talked with Tzu Hsi first of all for now she often spoke for the Emperor who was usually too ill to get out of bed. Prince Kung told her that though they had succeeded in keeping from any real showdown with the foreign powers so far, this time seemed to be almost over. The only thing the foreign nations respected was military power and they were very strong in this themselves with battleships and strange guns and with men trained in ways that the Chinese knew nothing about.

"Then the only thing to do is to arm our men so that they can attack the foreigners," Tzu Hsi said in her quick, definite way.

"Empress, if we do that who will be the first foreigners attacked? Ourselves. Have you forgotten that ours is an alien rule and that the rebels scattered through the land are only looking for a chance to get rid of the Manchu foreigners?"

Her mind went quickly from the national danger to the personal fear that her son might never become Emperor or she the Empress Dowager if events turned into catastrophe. She began to plan how an encounter with the foreigners could still be postponed. Such an encounter must not come until her son was old enough to take his seat on the Dragon Throne.

In the winter of that year the viceroy of Canton sent couriers to the capital to say that more foreign ships had arrived, that they lay at anchor in the river off Canton, and that this time some had brought envoys of high rank from England and that these demanded the right to approach the throne as representatives of an equal nation. When the Emperor heard the news he called his government together. Day after day they met and discussed what to do. In the night Tzu Hsi and the Emperor alone studied the written advices that had come from the day's audience and prepared their comment, only the decisions were truly hers. When Tzu Hsi finished the royal comment still proclaiming delay and making promises for the future, she sealed it with the imperial seal and next morning sent it out.

Once more Prince Kung came to her wild with anxiety.

Now the foreigners would not wait any more. Something had to be done at once. He told her he thought it possible, perhaps likely, that foreign ships would sail northward toward Peking, without waiting for permission, and bring their emissaries to the capital themselves. She paid no attention to what he said. She simply could not believe that any enemy would try to sail a thousand miles up along the China coast. Besides, her son was almost a year old and her mind was on a great birthday celebration she was planning for him.

While this celebration was going on and gifts from far and near were being received in the audience hall, couriers from the viceroy in Canton arrived again. The British emissary would not wait any longer. He was threatening to attack Canton. The viceroy would probably not be able to hold the city because the Taipings were stirring up feeling against the government.

Tzu Hsi still refused to be worried. Had they not succeeded in delaying action for all this time? Why not delay yet a little longer? Prince Kung reminded her that until now the British had been busy in India. Still Tzu Hsi would not be serious about Canton. The summer was coming on. They could send the viceroy word that the Emperor was too ill to be bothered and that they were taking him to the Summer Palace. When the summer was over they could discuss the question again.

By autumn the urgency seemed to have passed. Tzu Hsi congratulated herself. If only she could put off major decisions until her son was old enough to take his place on the throne and she became his regent, then all would be as she planned. By this time the Emperor was dangerously ill. He kept asking for her because she was the only person who could calm him and amuse him. She went to his bedside patiently, hoping if for a different reason than his, that he would still live for a long time.

Things went on like this all through the autumn and then

on a dark, cold day awful word came. The British foreigners had taken Canton, had made the viceroy a prisoner, and had established a government of their own in the city. They were sending their representatives to Peking to appear before the Emperor and present demands from their own Empress. In spite of herself Tzu Hsi was excited at the mention of the British Queen Victoria. She had sometimes imagined that a day would come when the two of them, herself and that Empress of the Western Hemisphere, might divide the world between them. She had to draw her mind back quickly to the serious news at hand. Prince Kung was reading the Canton memorial. He finished and looked at her. Was she still going to urge delay?

What else could she do? The Emperor was ill, the heir too young to act. There was nothing to do but to deny the foreign envoys entrance. When she put her worried thoughts into words, Prince Kung agreed and yet he believed that she did not understand how great the danger was.

"They will not be denied any more," he said quietly. "They will come and no one can hold them back, just as they took Canton and none could keep them from it."

Her eyes were on his face while he spoke and still she had no other answer for him. She simply shook her head and he arose and bowed and left the hall.

It was a bitter cold winter with unusually deep snow. Then the slow spring came on and at last another summer. Tzu Hsi longed to go to the Summer Palace but she dared not. Again Prince Kung came with bad news. The foreign ships were already moving up the coast in their battleships. Couriers came every day now to bring the latest reports. Soon the ships would arrive at Taku Forts only eighty miles from the capital. What was to be done?

The Emperor dragged himself from his bed and called an audience. The outcome of it was that the government would still not try to resist. Three men of high rank were appointed to go to Tientsin where the Taku Forts stood to negotiate with the English leader Lord Elgin when he arrived.

When Tzu Hsi heard this from her seat behind the dragon screen she cried out in protest. She called for war against the foreigners. But she had spoken when she should not have and no one paid any attention. The three men went to Tientsin and accepted papers leading to a treaty to be signed a year later. It would permit the British, the French, the Americans, and the Russians to have ministers of their governments in Peking and their traders and missionaries to travel wherever they liked. Hankow far inland was to be a new treaty port where foreigners and their families could live protected by their countries' laws. The treaty was to be signed in Tientsin and take effect in 1858.

Tzu Hsi had been defeated. Now she knew she could not do anything to change the decision made. She would still try indirect ways of influencing events. She took every opportunity to keep in close touch with the Emperor, she tried to please him in every way she could, and she made him trust her more and more. Then she led him to speak to Prince Kung. Why not send ministers to Canton offering the white men bribes, suggesting that when the year had passed the treaty be signed not in Peking but in Shanghai, so meeting them halfway? The forts at Taku were also strengthened with guns bought from the Americans. There must be strong resistance. If the foreigners would not accept the bribes and the suggestion to sign the treaty in Shanghai then the forts would be ready for battle. Although no one said anything openly, everyone knew that the Emperor's strategy grew out of Tzu Hsi's ideas.

In early summer word came by courier that the foreign ships were sailing for Tientsin. They were already far north of Shanghai. This was the foreigners' answer to the compromise offered. At the Taku Forts the imperial armies were strong and their men had been offered rewards. They fought off the foreign ships successfully. Three of the ships were destroyed and three hundred men were killed. The white men had to retreat without the treaty being signed. But Prince Kung was still uneasy. He could not believe that the foreigners had given up. They would be back, he declared.

He seemed to be wrong for a whole year passed quietly. The Emperor and his court went to the Summer Palace for the hot season. They had scarcely reached there when in July couriers hurried to tell them that two hundred foreign vessels had reached the port of Chefoo, not far from Tientsin, landing twenty-thousand armed men ready to invade the capital.

The terrified Emperor ordered a wise old nobleman to go immediately as an emissary of the court and make any promise at all that would delay the attack. Tzu Hsi was horrified. Had they not won in the earlier attack at the Taku Forts? Why give in so easily? She began to persuade the Emperor to try some other way of delaying a showdown. She suggested an ambush and at last the half-sick, fearful Emperor agreed. She reminded him of a Mongol general who had once before this defended the capital from rebels.

"Let him lead the ambush," she begged. "He is brave and resourceful," she whispered leaning against the Emperor and softening his resistance. The Emperor yielded to her suggestion. Not daring to tell Prince Kung or anyone, he sent this Mongol captain orders to prepare to lead his men against the white men, taking them by surprise.

It had been arranged that the French and the English emissaries were to meet the official representative of the imperial court at a certain time and place. At that moment they appeared carrying a white flag of truce. The Mongol general who was watching with his men fell on the foreign leaders and captured them. Then they attacked the troops with them and seized them and tortured many of them. The flag was trampled in the dust.

Word of the great Chinese victory was carried quickly back to the capital. The Emperor could not praise Tzu Hsi enough for her scheme and he ordered seven days of feasting in celebration of the great success. In the meantime the foreigners were angrily gathering for battle. They had been betrayed in good faith. They attacked the Mongol general and his men, quickly put an end to them, and marched on Peking. When this awful news reached the Emperor he ordered all the imperial troops to go immediately to meet the enemy. They came face to face only ten miles out of the city. Here the battle was fought and the foreigners with their guns easily defeated the poorly equipped government soldiers.

The foreign troops came on. What were left of the imperial troops hurried back to the capital and as they came the terrible news spread. Thousands of people joined them until it was almost impossible for anyone to move through the terror-stricken crowds that filled the streets. Women wailed and children cried and panic reigned.

At the Summer Palace the Emperor and the consorts and the members of the court had to decide quickly how to save the royal family. The Emperor wildly suggested that he had better commit suicide by swallowing opium. Prince Kung was the only one who seemed sensible in the disordered fear. He suggested that an offer of truce be prepared and sealed with the imperial seal. While this was being delivered to the leader of the foreign forces, the Emperor, the heir, and the two Empresses should go to Jehol, an ancient city one hundred miles away in the next province on the north.

Tzu Hsi rejected the suggestion of leaving the capital. To her it seemed as though the Emperor would be deserting his people. She declared they should return to Peking and take whatever fate came. Prince Kung admired her bravery but he urged her to consider the danger more realistically. He suggested that it was not necessary to make the Emperor's going to Jehol such a significant matter. He would simply announce that the Emperor was setting out for Jehol on a hunting trip, and they should make this seem so by not hurrying away. They left five days later. When they had traveled almost a day's journey they looked back and saw smoke rising. The beautiful Summer Palace was on fire.

Emperor Hsien Feng never returned to Peking from Jehol. He died in the dusty ancient city, but before he died Tzu Hsi quickly prepared an imperial edict which declared that her son was the heir. She held the Emperor's hand so that he could press the imperial seal upon the parchment.

When the court was on its way back to Peking, an assassin tried to take the lives of Tzu Hsi and her son. Jung Lu discovered his plot in time and killed the man. It was a sign of how dangerous her position was, for she would be Regent until her son was old enough to be put on the throne. She would have to be wary and clever and pleasing, watching for every danger inside the court, and always alert to what the troublesome foreigners were planning. She was only twenty-six and her child was not quite six years old. Somehow she would have to hold the reins of power for ten full years.

It would have been one thing to try to rule a great country like China in peaceful times, but now rebellions were springing up in all directions. Hung, the Taiping leader, was in Nanking. Muslims were causing trouble in the southwest, and in the northwest a tribe called the Nienfei were causing a great deal of anxiety. Then there were always the white men mixing into the Taiping Rebellion and nibbling at the southern edge of China while looking envyingly at the Yangtze River Valley. Empress Mother Tzu Hsi decided to move strongly against the Taiping leader. She wrote an edict stamped with the imperial seal ordering an all-out attack on Hung. All of the able military men were to gather for the attack.

When this order had gone out she gave her son his imperial name—Tung Chih, or Imperial Peace. From now on her mind was on her son. She prepared for his reign in every way she could. She would not let herself think of Jung Lu whom she really loved and to safeguard her heart she arranged a marriage for him to one of her ladies-in-waiting, a sweet and good woman. He finally agreed to it but not because his own feelings had changed.

One day she found the boy emperor had been given a mechanical toy train. To her it was a symbol of the invasion of China by the West and she was very angry. She snatched it from him and when she found that her cousin, the Empress of the Eastern Palace, had gotten it for him she took revenge in cruel ways.

She could think of such small things and she could spend hours in her library studying history and learning to paint while important and dangerous problems were bothering her. The war against the Taipings still seemed without an end. She had to put her mind on this one thing—to crush the Taipings. Tseng Kuo-fan and Li Hung-Chang, two fine generals, were in charge of the imperial armies. Every day couriers, running in relays, brought her the latest news from Tseng Kuo-fan. At last the word she hoped for came. Nanking had been taken back and Hung, the leader, had been found dead beneath the palace.

When the years had passed so that the young emperor was sixteen, Tzu Hsi had to arrange a marriage for him. How like her own coming to the court it was! Six hundred beautiful girls were paraded before them and from these they chose one to be his consort and four to be his secondary wives. Now at last the time had come for Tung Chih to ascend the Dragon Throne as Emperor. She could retire from active duty. She began to dream of rebuilding the Summer Palace which she had loved very much. She drew up plans and began to say that it was to be the gift of her son to her. Prince Kung warned her that the government could not afford such a great expense but she paid no attention to him.

Tzu Hsi turned against the young Emperor's consort when she saw that he loved her. She was jealous of the young woman's power over him and she deliberately undermined their relationship when she found that the consort was almost as daring and clever as she. Things grew worse when she discovered that the Emperor was still as interested in Western things and people as when, as a child, he had longed for a mechanical train. She blamed her daughter-in-law for encouraging him in this interest. A time came when the young Emperor even received envoys from the West although he did not permit them in the royal throne room. Instead they were received in a pavilion which meant that they were not accorded full dignity. Tzu Hsi laughed to think that those foolish men did not know the difference.

Now a new danger appeared. Tzu Hsi's daughter-in-law was to have a child. If it were a son then that young woman would become the Empress Mother and Tzu Hsi would have lost her power. For the ten years while her son was growing up she had managed to keep the empire safe for him and now everything seemed to be going wrong. He was insisting on closer touch with the foreign powers, he might have a son which would mean she was displaced by his wife, and outside dangers threatened again. Some Japanese ships had been wrecked on the shores of Taiwan and wild tribes living there had attacked them. Japan declared that these were Chinese tribes and in revenge she took control of that island so long held by China. The French had crept into Annam (Vietnam) and forced the King of Annam to sign away part of it to them on the pretext that bandits were interfering with their trade and Christian missions.

Tzu Hsi decided that with so many dangers threatening the empire she must take over the reins of government herself once more for Tung Chih was less and less interested in his responsibilities and more and more involved in his pleasures. As though she had been guided by fate Tung Chih was just then suddenly taken ill with smallpox and died. Tzu Hsi remembered sadly how she had not let him have that small toy, the mechanical train, and she was full of remorse. He had died so young, never having been the strong son she had hoped he might be. But she could not let herself think about the past for she had to think at once about who would follow him on the throne. If his consort's child were a son, he would be the logical heir. She would not have it so. She quickly chose a nephew of the former Emperor, the son of one of his brothers and her own sister. That very night she disguised herself and went to get him and bring him to the palace. Two days later she cruelly suggested suicide to her daughter-in-law and the desperate young woman took opium, killing her and the unborn child.

When this new child Emperor grew old enough he, too, loved foreign toys and this time Tzu Hsi let him have them remembering her own son and how because she had kept them from him, he had gone to others and been drawn away from her. The years were calm now under her rule while she waited again for an emperor to grow up. She began to have the new Summer Palace built, though she had to take the imperial navy funds to do it. Even the people agreed that it ought to be done because they had begun to lean on her as well as be afraid of her. Sometimes they called her by a loving nickname, Old Buddha.

At last the heir to the throne was seventeen and became the Emperor Kwang Hsu. Again he had to have a consort and

some secondary wives and again she ordered a review of
maidens chosen for their beauty and their wit. This young
man was more than ever interested in mechanical things, and
in foreign ideas but Tzu Hsi was old by now and her new
Summer Palace absorbed most of her interest. Let him have
what he wanted.

One day the calm was suddenly shattered when couriers
came running to say that Japan had taken Korea and destroyed the Chinese fleet. Tzu Hsi quickly blamed it on her
faithful general Li Hung-chang, declaring he had grown too
modern. He had started a merchant steamship company on the
Yangtze, had helped to build a short railroad, and he had
begun a weaving mill in Shanghai. She said that he was responsible for this outrage on the part of Japan. She went on to
blame him for the French in Annam and the Japanese in
Taiwan. It did no good to tell him to get all that had been lost
back again. Instead, Yuan Shih-k'ai, the Chinese general in
Korea, was driven away from there while Japanese landed
on the mainland and marched toward Peking. They were only
stopped by the embarrassing Treaty of Shimonoseki.

The young Emperor was interested in reform and though
Tzu Hsi tried to control him and weaken him in every way she
could, he issued statements of his own. The famous Hundred
Edicts were intended to bring about reforms in an ordered
way. They suggested changes in the examinations for civil and
military service, the founding of a new university where new
as well as the old subjects would be taught, the beginning of a
bureau of translations, and steps toward the building of rail-
ways and a new navy.

When Tzu Hsi heard of them she was horrified. This would
never do! She would not let them be put into effect. Jung Lu,
her old friend, came to warn her that a plot was being planned
to force her to accept change and that her nephew was behind
it. After all he had her own hot blood. She resisted all the

more. She secretly decided that now, no matter what the cost, the foreigners must be driven out of China.

First of all she had to control this young man who was getting out of hand. She made the Emperor practically a prisoner because of the controls she put on him and because of the way she humiliated him. But even as she did this, gradually so that it could scarcely be noticed, the foreigners grew more and more threatening and among her own people the desire for change grew stronger and stronger.

A showdown came. The young Emperor believed that Jung Lu, because he was close to Tzu Hsi, was his chief obstacle to bringing about changes. The Emperor secretly planned to have Jung Lu executed and he put the matter in the hands of the young military man Yuan Shih-k'ai. But Yuan told Jung Lu about the plan and so it reached Tzu Hsi. In retaliation she actually imprisoned the Emperor in a part of the palace, although she did not take away his title. This would have raised the question of succession and she wanted no successor. She had the power as Regent and she wanted to keep it. She ordered the chief leaders of the reform movement executed. She countermanded the edicts. She repressed progress in every way she knew.

But her plan did not succeed. The urge for change was swelling and growing. In a last desperate move Tzu Hsi listened to rumors that a secret society, called the Boxers because of the posture exercises they did, were immune to foreign bullets, and supported them in their increasing attacks on foreigners. Once she gave her approval of them, other groups of local militia and rowdies joined them. Their numbers swelled. In 1899 the Boxers began to persecute both foreign and native Christians in Shangtung Province. They killed a missionary. In another year a movement to sweep the country clean of the foreign religious organizations had begun.

In June 1900 an international military force arrived at

Taku Forts and stormed them to protect the foreigners in Tientsin and also to move on to Peking if necessary. When the Empress Dowager heard what was happening she ordered an attack on the Tientsin foreign concession and demanded that the foreign diplomatic representatives allowed by the treaty of 1858 be told to leave within twenty-four hours. She ordered that all aliens be done away with throughout the empire. Events telescoped. The German minister was killed. In another province a Roman Catholic bishop was murdered. In yet another province two hundred missionaries and several thousand Chinese Christians lost their lives.

Many times the local viceroys, officials, and citizens refused to carry out her orders. Instead, they protected the aliens and the Christians. Jung Lu was determined to bring Tzu Hsi to reason. He could not stop the coming of the foreign forces, but he could urge that steps be taken to check any further developments of war. He asked that the foreign ministers be properly escorted to the coast. Tzu Hsi would not hear of it. In the meantime the leaders of the foreign forces at Tientsin tried to explain that they were only interested in stopping the Boxers and in rescuing their own nationals who were being held prisoners or hostages in the capital. They did not think of themselves as being at war with China. Though they tried to make this clear, the Boxers could not be stopped and the foreign troops advanced on Peking to free their nationals.

Peking itself had by now been purged by the Boxers. The legations were still in a state of siege and they would not surrender so the Boxers had killed Christians wherever they found them, and had burned and ruined cities in their wild unruliness. Tzu Hsi was distraught with uncertainty as to what to do when word came that the foreign troops were advancing on the city overland from Tientsin. She still had to trust the Boxers and their claims to magic protection from foreign bullets. Jung Lu begged her to give them up, to use diplomacy, to come to a settlement. He was old now, he had suffered a severe stroke, but he was still loyal to her. At last, when he came to her and promised that if she and the Emperor and the consorts would be willing to escape, he would save the throne from the foreigners and so preserve the dignity of China, she agreed to go. When she had made the decision, she felt reassured and calm. She gave the order to leave and began to arrange everything quietly. The imperial seal must go with her but all her jewels and precious things would be hidden and left behind.

Empress Tzu Hsi and Emperor Kuang Hsu set out for the distant city of Sian, once called Ch'ang-an. Soon Jung Lu caught up with them and traveled with them. The journey took them ninety days. When they reached Sian the viceroy's palace became the royal palace. When couriers arrived from Peking every day Tzu Hsi held court just as though she were at home. She heard that the Western soldiers had occupied her beautiful new Summer Palace and had rampaged through the other palace courts.

Jung Lu was deeply worried about making a settlement with the foreign powers. He kept coming to Tzu Hsi and trying to talk things through with her. At last he said, "Majesty, you will have to punish the Boxers and all who helped them, before the foreigners will make any settlement."

"Is there not any other way to get free of these enemies of ours?" she begged him. She trusted him completely.

"There is not, Majesty," he answered gravely. He saw that she was still not willing. How could she be so proud? She was old now—they were both old.

"How can I turn on the people who have been so loyal to me," she almost whispered. Her eyes shone with the rarest of tears. "How can I!"

"You have to think of our country," he said. "You cannot

any longer consider this person or that, nor can you even think of yourself, Majesty."

The dusk came on and in the quiet court there was no sound except the evening song of a cicada in a giant tree. "You are right—always right," she whispered. "And so I must not stay here any longer but go back to my capital and begin to rule again."

That return was a royal procession. Now that the Empress Dowager had made up her mind to accept terms of settlement with the foreign powers, she was calm and gracious. To her real surprise she found that all through the countryside people came out in hoards to welcome her and to say how glad they were that she was returning to the throne. They called her Old Buddha affectionately and they brought gifts and they tried to get as near her as they could. They did not know how many problems there still were to be worked out. The fact that she was going back to Peking made them feel that everything would be as it had been before.

In her heart she had decided to show how progressive she could be. She would even ride on a train. It took thirty cars to accommodate the whole retinue and there was a great celebration at the temporary station built where they boarded to ride into the capital. Yes, she was going to change in every way she knew, and show them!

Jung Lu was still at her side. He was the one to worry over the cost of her triumphal return to the city. He was the one to worry over the terms of the settlement with the foreign powers, the Boxer Indemnity. He was the one to see that the changes she was trying to make had come when China had to pay a great price that she might have been spared if she had been willing to change sooner. She might have let the young Emperor lead the way, but she had not been willing.

She would never be willing for Kuang Hsu to play the part in China's history that he might have played. After Jung Lu

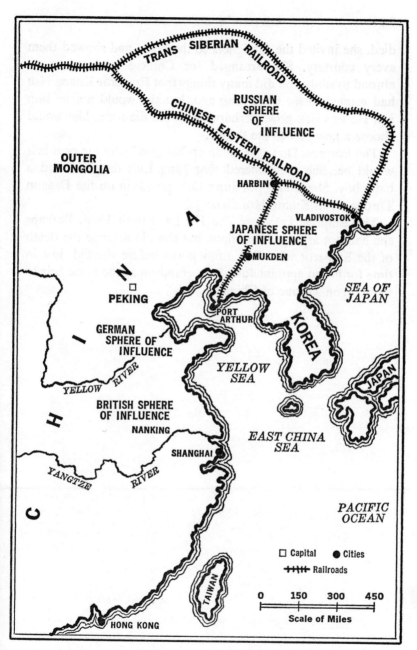

China in 1895–1905

died, she invited the foreigners to the court and showed them every courtesy. She arranged for Chinese students to go abroad to study and did many things that Emperor Kuang Hsu had wanted to see done long ago, but she would not let him act. He was sick now. Perhaps he would die soon. She would choose a new heir to the throne.

The Empress Dowager made up her mind who the new heir would be. She remembered that Jung Lu's daughter had a baby boy. She would put Jung Lu's grandson on the Dragon Throne when Kuang Hsu died.

The Empress Dowager Tzu Hsi lived until 1908. Perhaps she had not arranged that date, but she did arrange the death of the Emperor who died a few hours before she did, just in time for her to appoint Jung Lu's grandson as the royal heir to the Dragon Throne of China.

8

1866–1925

Sun Yat-sen

FOUNDER OF THE CHINESE REPUBLIC

The little village Choyhung where Sun Yat-sen was born was as rural a place as one could imagine. Its beaten-earth houses, some with threshing floors nearby, its half-dozen shops, a village school furnished with backless benches and narrow tables, its teahouse and market made it like any other small village in south China. It nestled among hills which seemed to shut it away from everything in the warm delta of the West River.

But this impression of isolation was misleading for Choyhung was near enough to the outside world, even before the beginning of the twentieth century, to feel its throb. It was close enough to the sea to catch its breezes. The great city of Canton which had been a port open to foreign trade for already twenty-five years was only forty miles away, and even in 1866 Canton was the center of revolutionary ideas. It was still full of talk about the Taiping Rebellion led by a Cantonese. Choyhung was even closer to Macao, a strange Old-World town, where the first Portuguese traders from Europe had taken hold of a piece of China three hundred years earlier and never let it go. Their ships dropping anchor in the shallow harbor and their stucco company houses made the port a foreign place.

Sun Yat-sen's father was a farmer and middle-aged by the time Yat-sen was born. The boy's mother was a country woman with the bound feet common then, and unable to read or write. Still, the farmer was a descendant of a duke who had migrated from the north during bad times. There were already other children in the family when Yat-sen was born. The one he would be closest to all through his life was a brother, Sun Mei, who was fifteen years older. In later life when Sun Yat-sen was known all over the world he would still say with a touch of pride that he was a *coolie* and the son of a *coolie*. The word comes from two Chinese ones which mean "bitter labor."

As soon as the small boy was old enough he went to the village school every day to study the classics. This meant memorizing them by reciting them aloud. When all the pupils did this at different pitches and tempos the uproar was enough to dumbfound anyone who did not understand what was going on. When a pupil had finished learning a passage by heart, he advanced to the schoolmaster's desk, placed his open book upon it before him, then turned his back and recited what he had learned. The only hope was to get the rhythm of the words because the classics were written in a kind of old-fashioned language which the boys did not understand, unless it was explained to them. Reciting with rhythm made the student sway from side to side so that his long braid of hair, or queue, swung like a pendulum behind him.

Just beyond the hills from Choyhung was a small harbor. Sometimes the boys wandered over there to watch the fishing boats come in. Occasionally a larger cargo junk dropped anchor for a day or two. If the boys were lucky they could get into conversation with a sun-browned seaman and hear tales of the outside world. Such tales added to an atmosphere that

Sun Yat-sen sometimes felt in his family circle—a feeling that the outside had reached in and taken something, or was pushing to get in. For a long time he did not know what this overhanging feeling was but as he grew older he gradually put things together and understood it.

In 1848 gold had been discovered in an American place called California. White men had come to China looking for laborers to work the gold fields. They wanted coolies who would be satisfied with very small wages. Two of Sun Yat-sen's uncles had gone and never come back and that explained the two rather sad-faced aunts who lived with the family. By 1852 there were supposed to be 25,000 Chinese working in the California gold fields.

The outside reached in with stunning suddenness one day when Sun Mei, Sun Yat-sen's older brother, emigrated to Hawaii. The Chinese called Hawaii the Sandalwood Islands because ships crossing the Pacific Ocean often stopped there for a cargo of the fragrant stuff and brought it to China where it was used to make joss sticks, or incense, and finely carved boxes and lacelike folding fans. Now Hawaii had begun to raise sugar cane and it needed laborers and managers for its cane fields. The sugar business attracted Sun Mei and he went in 1871.

Seven years later Sun Mei came home for a visit and to transact some business. Yat-sen was now not quite twelve. He was so excited by this man who was his brother that he hung on every word when they sat talking around the dining table. He could visualize everything that Sun Mei described.

Then, Sun Mei said, "I want to take Little Brother back with me. There are good schools there. He can study and help me, too." He looked at Yat-sen and smiled when he saw the brilliant color flood his face and his eyes shine with excitement. As if by chance Sun Mei jingled some coins in his pocket. He seemed to have any amount of money, Yat-sen thought—and now he wanted him to go to that wonderful place where he lived.

Yat-sen looked at his father quickly. He was the one who would have to answer. The farmer raised his brows and took a puff on his long-stemmed pipe before he answered. Then he stooped to knock the ash out of the bowl before he spoke.

"No," he said, "Yat-sen is too young. He already is always going over to the harbor and bringing back some wild story of the high seas. He needs to learn how to work here on the farm and forget nonsense. He is too young."

The answer was final and the sons knew it. Yat-sen sank back on the bench, his throat aching with sudden held-back sobs. And yet, he was relieved, too, because his brother was so rich and so self-assured that he was a little frightened of him, to tell the truth. Sun Mei was suggesting that the family move to a new house that he would build for them and he said that he would send money home regularly. Not until much later did Sun Yat-sen find out that on that very trip Sun Mei began a plan to ship immigrant workers back to Hawaii without cost to himself.

When Sun Mei came home again the next year to fill the first ship with workers, he asked to have Yat-sen go with the emigrants. Their father agreed this time and Yat-sen went aboard as though he were in a dream. It seemed impossible that he could be leaving home and going to the other side of the world. The ship was terribly crowded and he sometimes wished he had never come. The people around him were poor and some of them were seasick, but they seemed to feel that any other way of life was better than the one they were leaving behind. He soon forgot everything except that he was going to a place that belonged to America. He already knew a good deal about America and he had heard of a man named Abraham Lincoln who had wanted to set black people free.

The next three years began Sun Yat-sen's modern Western

education. His brother enrolled him in a British mission school called either The Bishops's College School or Iolani College. Actually, it was a primary school and all the school work was in English. Yat-sen spoke no English and he could not even understand it at first. But he learned quickly because he had to. He learned about two other important things. The first was music; he loved to sing and he soon was a member of the choir. He very much enjoyed wearing his robe and marching in and out for the religious services. The second thing Yat-sen learned about was Christianity. He soon wanted to be baptized a Christian but Sun Mei was very much against this.

Sun Mei was so worried that he wrote to the family in Choyhung and told them that Yat-sen had enough foreign schooling now and had better leave Hawaii and return home when he graduated. He would be going on seventeen by Chinese count, which adds an extra year, and it was time that a wife be found for him, he said. In his heart Sun Mei was afraid that the boy was getting radical, perhaps even revolutionary, ideas. Some of the talk he brought back from school certainly sounded strange.

Sun Yat-sen met both Britishers and Americans in Hawaii. He learned a good deal about America and the way it was governed. The life of the Hawaiian people, he saw, had been modernized by the oversight of the Americans. He dreamed about his country China and wondered how she could be helped to leave the past also and move into a new age.

When he returned home he was full of ideas and plans. Having forgotten what China was like during the years he had been away, when he landed and returned to Choyhung he was shocked by the backwardness of his own village. Impatient with everything, that impatience was bound to come out in some form before he had grown up enough to channel it in a constructive way.

One day, a boy whose family had once lived in Choyhung,

but had moved to Shanghai, was back in town attending a family funeral. Yat-sen listened while this boy told him all about the big city and how backward Choyhung seemed to him. They discussed religion, especially Christianity because of its revolutionary teachings. It seemed to them that the village temple where people still worshiped idols was just too ridiculous to be endured.

They wandered into the temple court one day and began to harangue the people who were there in larger numbers than usual, because it was a feast day. Yat-sen announced to the crowd that the images were not gods and that for anyone to worship them was simply a silly, superstitious practice. To demonstrate how stupid he thought the images were, he went to one and broke off its finger. He went on to others and defaced them, too. When news of what was happening began to spread, the villagers all came running. Someone went for the village Fathers, or Council. They held a very grave meeting and decided that Yat-sen's father would have to pay the costs of repairing the idols and that Yat-sen would have to leave Choyhung.

Although Yat-sen had not thought of the trouble he might bring on his father, he was glad to leave the village. A few months in the dull little place was more than enough for him. He wanted to go on with his schoolwork, but where? Hong Kong, of course, was the answer. There were British mission schools like the one he had attended in Hawaii and others to carry him on further, as well.

In Hong Kong he went to enroll in a British mission school and was accepted. In a building where a day school under an American mission was being run he found a room in which to live. There he met a young man, Dr. Charles R. Hager, who had just arrived from the United States and could not speak Chinese. Since Yat-sen had learned English in Hawaii, the two of them got on well. Sun Yat-sen even took Dr. Hager to

Choyhung for a visit to meet his family. The incident of idol-breaking seemed all but forgotten.

The friendship between Sun Yat-sen and Dr. Hager inevitably brought up the question of baptism again. One day Yat-sen said that he was ready to be baptized at any time. The American asked, "Why not now?" Soon after that he arranged a simple service in the school and Sun Yat-sen became a church member on the basis of his religious belief. This step was much more important in his life than it may have seemed at that time. It meant that he had broken with the whole tradition of his family and that he was ready to go forward in his own way into a new and revolutionary life.

First of all, he must have more education. In 1884 he applied to enter Queen's College, a good preparatory school in Hong Kong. This institution was an important choice because it required a student to study both Chinese subjects and Western ones and to meet the standards of both if he were to graduate. His time at Queen's gave Sun Yat-sen a classical Chinese background as well as a modern education that often surprised people who got acquainted with him later. Most of the young students wanted only the Western variety of education. The background in European and American history and literature was also to be important to him in the years just ahead.

Sometime during his first year at Queen's College, Sun Yat-sen's father died. After a suitable period of mourning, Yat-sen was married to a girl his parents had chosen as suitable for him. He only saw her when he went home on special occasions but she lived with his parents as a member of the family.

War broke out between France and China over Annam, later part of Vietnam. With no idea it was going to make so much personal difference to him, he joined other students in supporting a strike against French ships coming to harbor in Hong Kong. Somehow Sun Mei heard that Sun Yat-sen was involved in the student demonstrations. Added to the idol-breaking incident and Sun Yat-sen's becoming a Christian, it was too much. Sun Mei first threatened to stop sending money home, and then suddenly, he sent for Sun Yat-sen to come to Hawaii. He said that he needed him desperately to countersign some papers taken out in both their names.

Sun Yat-sen did not want at all to leave Queen's College after just one year, but the command of an elder brother was almost like the command of a father. He sailed for Hawaii in October. When he arrived he found that his suspicions were correct. Sun Mei wanted him to give up all of his connections with Christianity and to stop his radical activities, to stay away from strikes and demonstrations. The two brothers quarreled and Yat-sen declared that he wanted no more help from Sun Mei. He hated all the old Chinese family connections and responsibilities, he said, and he certainly could never follow in the steps of his forefathers. He wanted to be free.

He was free—but he had no money, not even enough to get back to China. Some of the Chinese Christians in Honolulu banded together and raised it, saying now that he had declared himself one of their group he ought to prepare himself to become a Christian minister. There were no theological seminaries in the southern part of China so that when Sun Yat-sen reached home again, he could not do what they wished. But he was impressed with the service to his people which Christian missionary doctors were doing, just as he had been impressed by mission schools where he had been receiving his education. Finally he decided that he could become a doctor and in that way satisfy both the wish of Chinese Christians in Hawaii and his own wish to help the Chinese community.

Between 1886 and 1892 Sun Yat-sen managed to get a full medical training. He established a small hospital in Macao and when the later regulations forbade that, he moved it to Canton. Although he was an able doctor his mind was still on the political condition of his country. While Sun Yat-sen was in medical school, he became reacquainted with the boy who years earlier had been involved in the idol-breaking episode with him. Now they often talked about a revolution. A third young man joined them and they formed a small, secret revolutionary society of their own.

Although Dr. Sun was now practicing medicine, he dreamed of a worldwide network of overseas Chinese who would support a revolution in China to rid the country of the alien Manchu dynasty in Peking which still ruled the empire, and of setting up a Chinese republic patterned after the United States. In 1894 he and his boyhood friend decided to present a memorial or statement to the viceroy in Peking asking for certain changes in government and outlining a program which seemed desirable for China. They prepared this carefully and traveled north. To their dismay they were not able to get near enough the viceroy to present it in person but had to give it to a lower official. This did not calm the young men. On the contrary, Sun Yat-sen was more determined than ever to move toward change. He went on to Hawaii and there he found enough young Chinese to establish the *Hsin Chung Hui* which means Prosper China Society. At least he now had a beginning of the world-wide society of which he dreamed.

The plan for this society took hold of Dr. Sun more and more. "Surely these Chinese living in foreign countries must be anxious to change their own country and make it into a modern nation; surely they want to get rid of the Manchus!" he kept telling himself. But, he was sure, too, that the only way a change could come was by a revolution. He had to be certain that those who joined the society would be willing to commit themselves that far.

He had wanted to travel on to the United States from Hawaii, but now it seemed that the first revolutionary step was to be taken back in Canton. The first thing, he decided, was to seize the provincial government headquarters in Canton. One night Sun Yat-sen and some of the young men who gathered around him attempted to seize the headquarters but their plans did not connect properly. The guns and dynamite they had ordered from outside of China never reached them. Customs officials discovered the guns hidden in barrels of cement. The plan collapsed.

Sun Yat-sen escaped to Hong Kong with a price on his head. The failure of the take-over was the worst thing that could have happened because from now on he was a marked man. He needed a disguise at once. He stepped into a barber shop and had his queue cut off and his hair trimmed in Western fashion. To his own surprise he found that now he looked much more Japanese than Chinese. He went out and quickly bought a regular business suit like most Japanese men wore in their offices although they might relax in Japanese *kimono* at home. Now feeling self-confident, he believed that he could pass without recognition anywhere.

Cutting off his queue was more than a change of hair style, it was the sign of a real change in Sun Yat-sen himself. He was no longer one of the Chinese educated class, those who went about in black skull caps and long silk gowns, but a modern man with modern ideas.

The escape to Hawaii was completed without any trouble. Even Sun Mei scarcely recognized him! While in Hawaii, Sun Yat-sen called the Prosper China Society together. Although some new members joined it, many of them were afraid because of what had happened in Canton. They had not expected him to be *that* much of a revolutionary! In a few months Sun Yat-sen planned to go on to the United States to find money and support for what was crystallizing as a plan for full-scale revolution against the Manchu dynasty.

Back in Choyhung things were happening fast. News of Sun Yat-sen's part in the attempt to seize the provincial government headquarters in Canton had been linked up with his ancestral village and then with his family. His relatives were terrified that they would be punished for his part in this event, as well as for the old image-breaking incident. When Sun Mei heard of this he became furious with his younger brother.

"You put your own big ideas before everything—even your own mother and family! You will risk their very lives for the sake of what you think of as saving China! Who is to look after them? You? Never! You think only of yourself and your plans."

Sun Yat-sen heard what his brother was saying but it all seemed so far away. Even the fact that he now had a son, Sun Fo, and two little girls seemed unreal. His brother was right, of course, for he did put China's destiny before everything personal, but he believed that was what he ought to do.

"I shall at least fulfill my duty as the oldest son," Sun Mei went on. "I, at least, have done well and I can afford to take care of my own."

Sun Yat-sen waited. What was his brother going to say next?

"I shall bring them all here where I can see that they do not suffer because of a vagabond revolutionist!"

Sun Yat-sen took a deep breath of relief. Nothing better could happen. As the father of the Chinese Republic he could not possibly put his mind on family matters. But he thought it better to say very little about it. Sun Mei could not really grasp the significance of the Revolution.

"I shall send word that a young man who has gone from here to his old home in Choyhung to get himself a bride is to bring the Sun family here," Sun Mei went on with a touch of pride. When at last the family all had arrived in Hawaii, Sun Yat-sen was delighted.

He was especially pleased with his son who was a bright little schoolboy. Now he could go on to his own important affairs and never need to worry about the safety of his family.

At last he pushed on toward San Francisco. Because he was still a Chinese criminal with a price on his head, there were difficulties in his way. Also, the United States Greary Exclusion Act was in force against Chinese immigrants. To gain entry into the United States he might try pretending to be Japanese. Or he might say that he had been born in Hawaii and was an American citizen. He landed without difficulty and was even so self-confident that his disguise was effective that he had a photograph of himself taken.

He stayed in the United States for three months traveling from one little Chinese community to another, trying to elicit their help for the Revolution. It was a disappointing undertaking. He found that most of the Chinese were conservative. They had worked hard to get into businesses where they could make a living and they were not at all ready to upset their security by getting themselves involved in dangerous activities.

While Dr. Sun was moving about freely in America, the Chinese Minister in Washington, D. C., found out that he had come to the United States and that he was planning to go on to London. He cabled the Chinese Minister in London, alerting him. Soon after he landed in England, Sun Yat-sen realized that he was being watched. Ten days after he arrived he was accosted and taken to the Chinese Legation. It looked as if he might be held indefinitely while some way of getting him back to China as a political prisoner was worked out.

Sun Yat-sen was truly desperate. He was not allowed to contact anyone outside. Even his British friends whom he had known in Canton and with whom he had been staying before he was arrested did not know what had happened to him. He tried writing notes, weighting them with coins, and dropping them from the windows of the room where he was confined. They failed to reach anyone for they were actually caught by an outjutting ledge of roof. At last he began trying to persuade the English servant, who brought him food and carried in coal to keep his fire burning, to help him. Although he was not easily frightened, he had reached the stage where he could not sleep and he was distraught with anxiety. He could imagine all sorts of terrible punishments not only for himself but for the others who belonged to the revolutionary society.

One day he said to the servant, "The Emperor of China wants to kill me because I am a Christian, when really I and my party only want to get some good government for my country. My life is in your hands." He waited while the man stood miserably before him, uncertain as what to do. "Unless you let my friends know that I am being held, I shall certainly be killed."

Finally persuaded, the English serving man began to carry notes in and out in his coal scuttle. Even then it seemed difficult to get them delivered to the right places. At last, late one night, Dr. Sun's old Canton friends heard a slight sound at their front door and opened it to find that a note from him had just been pushed under it. They were both overjoyed and astounded. First, they tried to bring legal pressure to bear on the case and when that became tied up in red tape they gave the story with all its dramatic episodes to the press.

Reporters rushed to the Chinese Legation. Headlines blazed. The British Prime Minister was drawn into the affair. He courteously advised the Chinese Legation that in holding Dr. Sun it was infringing on British law and that they should release the revolutionary at once. Dr. Sun was set free in a spotlight of publicity.

The experience had been an important one. While a prisoner, he had thought over things a great deal. He had had to depend on religion or go mad. He had found an inward peace that would not leave him in the future, no matter what happened. Now he often went to the great library in London and

read political theory and history. He met some Russians there
and they discussed Marxism. These experiences led him to
think through the meaning of the Revolution more and more
carefully.

But he had no intention of changing his plans at all because
of what had happened. He was now not only a marked man in
China but a marked man all over the world. He started for
Europe to get in touch with young Chinese there, most of
whom were university students. What he had been reading and
what came out in discussions with them combined with his
own ideas. He formulated a basic plan for China's new government and development, calling it The Three Principles of
the People.

Two years had passed since he left China and now he dared
to attempt to go back. In 1899 he reached Japan and found
many young Japanese were interested in his ideas. European
culture was sweeping the islands and modernizing them. In
Japan he waited and consolidated his plans and ideas. China
had many secret societies and he made connections with some
of them that he thought might help his cause. Instead of going
across to China he made a second world tour before trying it
and elicited the help of Chinese secret societies wherever he
went. He was still laying his foundation.

In 1905 he was back in Japan. He reorganized the old Prosper China Society into the T'ung Meng Hui, or Chinese Revolutionary Society. The night this was accomplished was never-
to-be-forgotten. He had found that there were forty branches
of the Prosper China Society around the world and now four
hundred men attended the meeting when it was made into
an openly revolutionary organization. Dr. Sun had an extraordinary gift for speaking. He could feel inspiration take
hold of him. Ordinarily calm and quiet-voiced, far from being
impressive in appearance, when he began to make a public
speech his voice took on timbre and his whole person seemed
to catch fire. On this night the young men hung on to his

words and when the public address was over they crowded around him, ready to dedicate themselves to almost anything he suggested. One of the young men was a Chinese student in the Tokyo Military Staff College. His name was Chiang Kai-shek.

The formation of the T'ung Meng Hui involved for the first time the true intellectual leaders of Chinese thought in the work of the revolution. From this time on, Dr. Sun began to make definite plans to overthrow the Chinese government. The attempts had to begin in Canton where there was strong support from secret societies and where revolutionary ideas caught on easily. The T'ung Meng Hui was flourishing there. Yet, in spite of all this, in the next five years attempts failed twelve times. They always turned into small, local affairs. The Revolution still did not have enough good leaders, adequate funds, or proper communication with like-minded groups, or even within itself.

An accident hurtled China into the Revolution of 1911. A network of secret planning had been spreading steadily through the years because the Chinese people were more and more eager to get rid of the Manchu rulers. Learning new things from the West, they were eager for change. The revolutionaries in the triple cities of Hankow, Wuchang, and Hanyang, known as Wuhan, six hundred or more miles up the Yangtze River from Shanghai, hired bomb-makers to prepare munitions for the day when the real outbreak would come. These men worked in the basement of a house in the Russian concession, an area granted to a foreign power by treaty in certain ports. On the night of October 9 a bomb accidentally exploded in Hankow. It alerted the government guards. Now there was no holding back the Revolution. It had to go forward at once or fail completely.

At the time, Dr. Sun was in the United States on another trip to raise money and to weld the overseas Chinese into stronger support for the revolutionary cause. He received a coded telegram one day but his code book had been shipped ahead to Denver in his baggage. There was nothing to do but wait until he caught up with it, which would take about two weeks. When he finally arrived in Denver and decoded the telegram he discovered that it was a desperate appeal for funds.

The very next morning while having breakfast in a restaurant a newspaper headline transfixed him. WUCHANG OCCUPIED BY REVOLUTIONISTS, it said. What had happened? He knew that this was sooner than planned. As he continued to travel he saw the headlines everywhere. Then the story of the accident became known. Dr. Sun started home but he was still under pressure to get funds, or the assurance of funds. In England and in France he succeeded in getting the support of the two countries for the new Chinese government instead of their continuing to support the empire.

A wildly enthusiastic crowd welcomed Dr. Sun in Shanghai. Failures were forgotten. The great day had come. Nanking was the capital of the new government and here Dr. Sun was elected Provisional President in December 1911. But a boy emperor was still on the throne in Peking, the old capital. The premier of that Manchu government was Yuan Shih-k'ai, a conservative, and he began peace talks with Dr. Sun in Nanking. Some of the revolutionists were terribly worried. Did Dr. Sun not see that Yuan was trying to destroy all that they had worked for? Then, unbelievably, Dr. Sun agreed to let Yuan Shih-k'ai take his place as President! He would rather put his effort into building up a big railway system for China, he declared. When some of his men complained to him, Dr. Sun said, "What are you so anxious about? Yuan has promised to remove the emperor and go on with the establishing of the republic." Yuan agreed to all of Dr. Sun's suggestions and made a magnificent statement on democracy to the republic.

One of the points in the agreement Dr. Sun had made with

Yuan Shih-k'ai was that the capital should be located in Nanking rather than Peking. Soon Yuan decided that he did not want to do that after all, but he only said that he would move the capital south after he stabilized the situation in the north. As outbreaks continued, the move was delayed again and again.

In spite of this problem and the fact that two key revolutionary leaders were killed near Peking, Dr. Sun felt that the Revolution had been successful. China was a republic. Now all that was left to be done was to work out the stages of development which he had outlined in his Three Principles of the People. These stages were really based on Abraham Lincoln's "of the people, by the people, for the people." In adapting them to the Chinese situation, Dr. Sun stated it in this way. "The people are to have, the people are to control, the people are to enjoy." Put even more simply, the three principles were Nationalism, Democracy, and the People's Livelihood.

The first stage, he felt, had been accomplished. Now the second must begin. Democratic government must be started. The T'ung Meng Hui was reorganized as the Nationalist Party, or the Kuomintang.

In that year Dr. Sun also re-married. The new Madame Sun was Soong Ching-ling, the second daughter of a well-known family in Shanghai, and sister of Soong Mayling who would become Madame Chiang Kai-shek. She had been active in the revolutionary group, as had her whole family, and she admired and then fell in love with the middle-aged revolutionary leader.

But Dr. Sun had trusted Yuan Shih-k'ai too far. The old military man had no intention of changing China into a republic. Yuan openly proclaimed the re-establishment of a monarchy and himself as emperor in 1916. There was nothing to do but to start a new revolution.

Once more the revolution began in Canton. The revolutionaries succeeded in setting up a military government in 1917 and elected Dr. Sun Generalissimo. He at once began to plan a Northern Expedition against Peking. The north and the south would have to be joined before unified government could be started. Although Dr. Sun had always been thoughtless about personal danger and although his plans were now so audacious that they took the breath of many of his followers, he did not look the part of a generalissimo at all. He was rather small, his expression soft and gentle. He spoke quietly except when he was making a public speech. He impressed people as a scholar or teacher rather than as rebel with fiery thoughts of overthrowing governments.

In 1923 Chiang Kai-shek, the young military student who had first heard Dr. Sun speak in Tokyo and had there joined the T'ung Meng Hui, came to Canton. He had taken part in some of the revolutionary activities in Shanghai. By this time Dr. Sun had become acquainted with a Russian envoy to China named Adolf Joffe. Dr. Sun was desperate for foreign help for his cause and Russia seemed willing to give it. The revolutionary forces, he realized, needed much better military preparation than they had. He sent Chiang Kai-shek to Moscow to study military techniques so that he could come back to train men for the continuing revolutionary fight.

The year after Chiang Kai-shek returned to Canton, Dr. Sun launched his Northern Expedition. He had to turn back because some of the men in Canton whom he had trusted, even though he was warned against them, sabotaged his plans. Something had to be done. He issued a manifesto calling on all provinces to help get rid of the Peking regime. He sent out his own generals against special points where he would be opposed. Along the West River in the province where Canton stood, Chiang Kai-shek attacked the man who had sabotaged the expedition. These efforts were encouraging.

Then a sudden turnover in Peking brought a dramatic

change. A military man, Feng Yu-hsiang, suddenly took control of Peking by a trick. He had been allied with the Revolution so that it seemed to be its victory. Feng set up a provisional revolutionary government and invited Dr. Sun to come to Peking in order that the country could at last be unified.

It was impossible for Dr. Sun to turn down the invitation although some of his party were afraid that it might be a dangerous plot. He and Madame Sun started for Peking by way of Japan. At every port enormous crowds of young people waited for him. He had to speak again and again. Although he had not been well for a long time, suddenly he became dangerously ill. Still he would not give up and he spoke even though his face was ashen.

It was a triumphant journey to Peking. Dr. Sun sent out messages saying that he was going to the north to convene the national assembly, to abolish imperialism, and to surrender the federation in the south, of which Canton was the center, for the cause of a united China. He was full of hope, but as he journeyed on he was in great pain. The newspaper men noticed it even while he was making speeches.

Because he was so ill, they stopped in Tientsin on the way to Peking. Representatives from Peking called on him there. When he heard the Peking government's plans for reorganization he realized that they had ignored the points upon which they had agreed earlier. Still he would not give up. After a ten-day rest he went on to Peking in a special train coach. Once there he had to rest again for ten days. Now he knew that the trip north had been a defeat rather than a triumph. Everything he learned showed that the government was in the hands of the monarchy, that there would be no true reconstruction in the proposed reorganization conference. One day he roused himself out of deep pain to cry out furiously that no members of the Revolutionary Party, the Kuomintang, were to take part in the reorganization conference.

It was the last order he gave. When he was dying a few weeks later, those around him begged him for a statement to the country for which he had worked so hard. But he believed that he had been completely defeated; that everything was lost. All that encouraged him at that last hour was the news from Canton. Young General Chiang Kai-shek had defeated their old enemy in a brilliant attack. Canton itself was in good hands and it seemed that points further south were being taken over by a new revolution.

Dr. Sun agreed to sign statements prepared for him. They became his will and thousands of children all through China would memorize them while they gazed with respect and worship at a large photograph of the Father of the Chinese Republic hanging in hundreds of schoolrooms in the years to come.

Dr. Sun died on March 12, 1925. He was buried in a temporary grave in the Western Hills near Peking while a magnificent mausoleum was prepared for him, on Purple Mountain outside Nanking. His body was moved there in 1929 and an impressive funeral was conducted to which dignitaries came from all over the world.

9

1886–

Generalissimo

Chiang Kai-shek

LEADER OF EXILED NATIONALIST CHINA

"Why won't you study and be a good pupil! Why must you always cause trouble at school?" the Chinese mother asked her eleven-year-old son, Chiang Kai-shek. He stood before her, his face set stubbornly and his eyes dark with rebellion. He was dressed for school, his long hair smoothly braided in a queue.

"Your father told you so often how he wished he could have had an education so he wouldn't have had to be only a wine and salt merchant." She sighed and smoothed down her stiff, dark cotton jacket. "He begged you to study hard—and now you only cause trouble. Tricks, refusing to work, always late—I have only complaints from Teacher Wu." She stopped and tried to get his eye, but he would not look at her.

He did not answer. Everything his mother had said was true. His father, who had died two years earlier, had often said just these things—but he still hated school. He could not keep his mind on memorizing dull passages from ancient writers; his thoughts went off in all directions.

Now he turned on his heel and left as if to go to school, but he only started in that direction. The moment the house was out of sight he branched off and went toward the edge of the village.

His village of Chikow in Chekiang, a southern province of China, nestled among high, abrupt hills and deep valleys with rushing streams. It was not far from the important seaport Ningpo nor very far from famous Hangchow. But to the boy, it was a world in itself. This morning he trudged on until he had left the village with its marketplace and tea shop and a half dozen small stores entirely behind him. When he had come to a spot shaded by the rising mountains and cooled by fine mist from a waterfall, he sat down on a rock to think of what to do.

He stayed there for what seemed a long time, idly dropping leaves into the stream and watching them swirl away, or his eyes following a dragonfly that hovered over the water, glinting like a sliver of metal caught in reflected sunlight. He saw it all, and yet he was not trying to see it. He was deciding what to do about school.

He hated it, and yet if he did not get an education, what would happen to him? He would have to go into the Chiang family business of salt and wine. He would have to sit behind a high counter all day and talk to merchants who came to see him, and order a couple of clerks around as they waited on customers. There was another possibility. He could keep on enduring school until he was in his teens and then run away and join the army. He would like that, but it would surely kill his widowed mother. Chinese people thought that soldiers were the lowest level of society. Only those who were no good for anything else became soldiers, they said. Even Confucius had long ago declared that a blacksmith would as likely use fine metal to make nails as a country call its good men to be soldiers.

One thing was certain. He would never be a merchant. That meant he had to go back to school until he was old enough to think over the question of being a soldier some more. He picked up a stone and threw it hard at a small green frog sitting on a rock enjoying the cool spray from the falls. He missed his target but the frog jumped and swam to reappear, blinking at him, on another rock. Kai-shek did not smile. Instead, he turned away and started slowly back to town, his face set in unhappy determination.

He managed to pass the primary grades but there was no school in Chikow to take him further in his studies. He would have to go to a larger town for that where Chiang relatives lived and had a wine and salt store. Kai-shek's mother arranged for him to board with them and help them after school. In this way he would be learning the business while he was studying, and if he failed to pass his exams he would be ready to become a storekeeper. Chiang Kai-shek hated this arrangement but he was eager to go to a larger town.

Although he was still a problem to his teachers and had no close friends among the students, he began to like some of his subjects. He enjoyed stories of ancient heroes who won great battles. He particularly admired a man named Yo Fei who had lived in the twelfth century. Yo Fei had turned the northern barbarians away at the very gates of Hangchow, then the capital of a southern Chinese kingdom, only to be betrayed and killed by a wicked Minister and his wife. Chiang knew that a monument to Yo Fei stood in Hangchow at this very time.

During the years that he was in the higher school, Chiang Kai-shek discovered that there was a military academy in Tokyo, Japan, where some Chinese students were accepted. Perhaps . . . but he must not think of that until he had finished his schooling.

Helping in his relatives' store he found almost unbearable.

He did it so badly that they scolded him again and again. At last they threatened to send him back to Chikow if he did not improve. He did just a little better in his work, but even so he found ways of escaping to the tea house to listen to discussions among men and even some of the older students from his school. They talked about the Taiping Rebellion which had swept the Yangtze Valley thirty or so years before he was born and of the man who had started the revolution and tried to set up a new government with some strange religious background. They talked about treaties that followed wars with foreign countries and gave those countries special rights, or concessions, in certain port cities. They talked about the Chinese-Japanese war which had occurred at the beginning of the century. They talked about the present Manchu government in Peking and how the Manchus were foreigners and should not rule the Chinese. Then they mentioned a man named Sun Yat-sen who had been trying to overthrown the Manchus. He had begun a revolt in Canton but had been caught and had had to escape. He went to Japan, to Hawaii, to America and then to England where he was held as a political criminal for a while. The boy overheard only snatches of these events but they were enough to make him study his history harder and to excite his imagination and make him dream of military adventures.

While he was at school, discovering more and more about his country's relation to the rest of the world, his mother arranged for him to be married to a village girl in the traditional Chinese way. He went home for this event when he was fourteen. After it was over he returned to school. It was all like a dream. It did not change his life at all.

To his whole family's surprise he graduated. His mother already had a plan for his future. "I want you to go to Hangchow to study to be a lawyer," she said. "That is a calling with prestige and many opportunities to make good money. In this way you will help the whole Chiang family rise higher in the world." She paused, not looking at him for fear his face would register displeasure. "I have talked to a man who knows just whom you ought to see."

The very thought of studying to be a lawyer made Chiang shudder, but he must not speak too soon, or let his expression betray him because he would like very much to go to Hangchow. He had never seen the famous city. After a moment he caught his mother's eye and said pleasantly, "That is a good idea. I shall be glad to go to Hangchow and look into learning law."

In that wonderful old city Chiang found the monument to Yo Fei and stood before it. China rarely honored her military leaders by monuments but here was one. Chiang went on to enjoy the pleasure spots on the edge of famous West Lake. Here he heard students arguing one evening. They were discussing plans to go to that very Tokyo military school he had heard of! He found that it was called the Tokyo Military Staff College. Instantly his own thoughts were clear. Of course, he would go there! His mother could not object because he would still be going to school. Students who applied there and were accepted had some of their expenses paid, too, it seemed. This would help persuade his mother for she was always straining to meet the extra expense he caused her.

When he went home and told her what he wanted to do, she finally agreed but she had not counted on his new ideas going as far as they did. The morning he left she caught her breath when he turned his back toward her. He had had his queue cut off! Before she had time to protest, he was gone. What did it mean? She had heard villagers talk about short-haired students who were followers of a dangerous man called Sun.

When Chiang started for Shanghai, from where he was to take a ship for Japan, it all seemed too good to be true. He was on his way to become a military man! Shanghai was unbelievable, too. He rode around the city in a rickshaw and marveled at the concessions with their broad tree-lined streets, which had been given to foreign nations by treaty. Ships from all over the world were at anchor in the river harbor. He enjoyed the mixture of Western and Oriental amusements which made the nights gay. But when he arrived in Tokyo and went to register at the Tokyo Military Staff College, he was rejected. They told him that he should first have attended a preparatory school in Paoting, a city in the northern part of China. After doing that he would have to be within a quota allowed Chinese students.

He dared not write home immediately about what had happened. What would his mother say about all the wasted travel money! Instead, he decided that he would look up other Chinese students and ask them to take him in so that he could enjoy Japan now that he was here. He also studied the Japanese language.

When he returned to China, a surprise was waiting for him in Chikow. His wife had given birth to a son. They named him Ching-kuo. Even yet this marriage seemed unreal, for he was still a student. He told his mother about the academy in Paoting. Entrance examinations for it were given in provincial centers all across the country and he could take his right near home. When he went to take the examinations he passed so easily that he surprised even himself. Of course, they were on military subjects which he loved.

He needed only one year's study at the Paoting school and he enjoyed it except for the fact that there were not many students from the south. Soon he discovered that he was the only one, even among the southern ones, who had his hair short. He was teased and almost ostracized because of his haircut and what they thought it signified—that he was a revolutionist. He had made no such decision; he was just revolting against things in his own life.

Final examination time at the Paoting Academy came and Chiang had no trouble in answering the questions. He knew that he had passed well, yet when he went to look at the list of graduates he did not see his name there! In a panic he hurried to the school's office to find out what was wrong. He had to fight his way up the line of authorities to get included in the quota for the Tokyo school. Why had this happened? Was it because the northern school was against any southerner, or were the school authorities afraid of his short hair? Never mind. He had shown them that he would not be intimidated that easily. At last in 1907, when he was almost twenty, he was ready to start for Japan again.

This time he was accepted at the Tokyo Military Staff College without any trouble. His ability to speak Japanese recommended him especially. Now he met other Chinese students who were interested in military careers. They looked at Japan and were excited about the way she was changing into a modern nation. Would China ever change, they wondered.

One of the young Chinese who became Chiang's good friend told him that Dr. Sun Yat-sen was in Tokyo working on his plans for the Revolution. One night in 1910 they went to a student meeting where Dr. Sun was speaking. The hall was crowded with short-haired young men. Dr. Sun did not seem impressive. "He looks like a middle-aged Japanese business man," Chiang said in a low voice to his friend. When Sun began to speak at first everyone had to strain to hear him, but as he got into his subject his voice took on a new resonance. It vibrated with life and emotion so that what had begun as a quiet talk became an oration.

Chiang Kai-shek listened carefully while Dr. Sun discussed China's situation and the only possible solution to it, revolution. Dr. Sun told about his world-wide revolutionary organization, the T'ung Meng Hui, made up of Chinese in many countries who were dedicated to the purpose of freeing China from her Manchu rulers and replacing the empire with a republic.

When the speech was over, there was a sudden stillness. Everyone seemed to be waiting for the next step. Dr. Sun asked all those who wanted to join his society to come forward and take an oath of allegiance to it. Chiang was carried away by what he had heard. He stepped forward with the others and repeated the words which made him a member of the revolutionary society, the T'ung Meng Hui.

During the four years that Chiang Kai-shek was in Japan, first attending the college and then, after he had graduated, serving in the Japanese Imperial Army by a special arrangement with Peking, he sometimes went back to China. Each time he had an errand taking him to the home of a man named Soong, in Shanghai. He discovered that Charlie Soong and his wife were Christians and had spent many years in America. They had five children. Two of their three daughters had graduated from American colleges and the youngest, Mayling, was still in the United States. Dr. Sun was an old friend of the family and often visited them. That was why he was always sending messages to them from Japan by anyone going to Shanghai.

On October 11, 1911, when Chiang was with the Japanese army, he was hurriedly summoned back to China. The Revolution had been precipitated accidentally when a bomb exploded and plans for the revolution were discovered. The only thing to do was to update the Revolution and plunge into it at once even though Dr. Sun was on a money-raising trip abroad. Everyone who could help was needed. Chiang left by ship for Shanghai at once. He went to the home of the young man who had introduced him to Dr. Sun and the T'ung Meng Hui in Tokyo, but he almost lost his life in getting there.

Chiang's military ability was put to the test immediately in the emergency. He took part in surprise attacks to save

Shanghai, and then to take Hangchow. After Dr. Sun returned
to China and was elected Provisional President of the Chinese
Republic in Nanking in December, 1911, Chiang became
more and more connected with the new government. He often
sat in on organizational meetings.

As he became better acquainted with Dr. Sun, he saw that
there were two different sides to the man. One was of a brave,
daring, hard-headed revolutionist; the other was of a naïve
dreamer who seemed to have no practical sense. The second
side now led Dr. Sun to accept peace proposals from the old
monarchical leadership in Peking in order to unify the country. Chiang and others warned him that this would result in the republic being betrayed and in a reversion to the
monarchy, but Dr. Sun would not pay any attention to the
warnings. What he had been told would happen soon took
place. Now he said that a second revolution had to be started
at once.

There was no time to organize this second revolution properly. It failed almost as quickly as it had begun and the revolutionary leaders including Chiang escaped to Japan. They
gathered at the Soong's Tokyo home. They were truly an exiled revolutionary government now.

In 1915 Chiang was back in Shanghai working with his old
student friend. They tried to take control of Shanghai away
from the Manchu government forces but the plot failed.
Chiang began to work for the Revolution secretly. When the
northern leader who had betrayed the Revolution died in
1916, Dr. Sun returned to Canton to start the Revolution all
over again. There he set up a military government to carry on
until it was possible to reestablish the republic. Many problems delayed him. Revolts failed. Warlords hampered him.
Strikes confused relations with the foreign powers. Students
became vocal about their country and went out on parades
against foreign aggression.

In 1921 Dr. Sun decided to start an expedition to Peking to take it in the name of the Nationalists, or the Kuomintang, who had replaced the T'ung Meng Hui. This action would unify the country. Chiang knew that an enemy of Dr. Sun's in Canton would sabotage the expedition and he tried to dissuade him. The doctor would not listen to the young military man. What made him think that just because he had become an officer in a military school and led a couple of coups, he could advise the founder of the Chinese Republic? He started the expedition.

While Dr. Sun was on his way north, Chiang Kai-shek's mother died in Chikow. He went home for the burial and proper period of mourning, which could be as long as three years, glad to get away from Canton. He knew that Dr. Sun was doing the wrong thing and that some calamity was approaching. Dr. Sun's old enemy warlord in the Canton area soon sabotaged his expedition and Dr. Sun turned back, admitting his failure. In Chikow Chiang waited. While he was there he decided to take out divorce papers to end his marriage to his childhood bride. They had not seen each other for years.

During the summer of 1922 while he was still in Chikow, his personal affairs were interrupted by a telegram from Dr. Sun. It begged him to come and help. Dr. Sun was aboard a small cruiser on the river near Canton and seemed to be a prisoner. Chiang hurried away, mystified about what had happened. When he arrived he found that Dr. Sun's old enemy had organized a rebellion in Canton and tried to capture Dr. Sun. Fortunately the doctor had been warned in time to escape. Madame Sun, one of the Soong sisters, had followed. They finally reached the ship which was hiding among foreign craft on the river.

Chiang spent five weeks with Dr. Sun on the little gunboat through blistering hot summer weather. They came to know each other well. Dr. Sun was surprised to see that the rather stiff, cold military man could unbend now to do any chore needed during those tiresome days. Sometimes Chiang had to disguise himself and go ashore to buy supplies. At other times he had to break up quarrels among the crew. He even swept and mopped the decks.

At last, with the help of the British Consul in Canton, Dr. Sun and his party escaped to Shanghai by way of Hong Kong. In Shanghai they often gathered at the Soong house. Although Charlie Soong had died in 1918, Mother Soong held the household firmly together. The youngest daughter, Mayling, had finished her college work brilliantly and returned to Shanghai. General Chiang had never seen anyone quite like her. She was pretty, lively, intelligent, and full of ideas about the future of China. He called on her often and when he went out of the city, they wrote to each other.

In 1923 a dramatic event changed Chiang Kai-shek's life. He had been having a discouraging time in Shanghai. There seemed to be no way to use his military calling, for the Revolution was faltering. He had begun to play with finances in Shanghai, hoping to be lucky and make a fortune. Instead, he went bankrupt, and on the advice of friends he left the city and went to Dr. Sun in Canton to see if there were some way he could help.

Meanwhile Dr. Sun had been talking with Russians in Shanghai and he believed that their country was the best foreign nation to turn to for help. She certainly seemed ready to assist in every way. Dr. Sun had come to the conclusion that Russian advisors were right in saying that the Revolution would never succeed unless it had better military power. When Chiang Kai-shek turned up, he seemed just the answer.

"I want you to go to Moscow and study Soviet military techniques," he said to Chiang almost the moment they faced each other.

"Moscow!" Chiang could not collect his ideas about it so quickly. But he was interested in all military tactics and he thought that at last Dr. Sun might be seeing that the Revolution needed better trained military forces and leadership. "I'll go," he said after only a moment's hesitation. The experience would be interesting and it might turn out to be useful for China.

Chiang Kai-shek was gone a little less than a year. When he returned he brought back promises and plans. Russian leaders had suggested starting a military academy in China and offered to send a number of their instructors and advisors to help. The academy was to be near Canton.

Dr. Sun was enthusiastic about this plan and the Whampoa Military Academy was begun as quickly as possible. Qualified students were recruited from all over the country, only there were too many of them. The number to be registered was set at three hundred; fifteen hundred applied. At last, plans were stretched and five hundred were accepted. The Academy was a success from the first. Thirty or so Russian advisors came and helped to make it efficient.

Dr. Sun was still impatient to begin an expedition to Peking. In 1924 he laid plans to start out again but events took an unpredictable turn. Peking was captured in the name of the Revolution by a northern general, Feng Yu-hsiang, who had allied himself with the revolutionaries but had tricked them. Now he invited Dr. Sun to come north so that Canton and Peking might be joined at last. Although some of the southern leaders were suspicious, Dr. and Mrs. Sun started north in a great cavalcade, by way of Japan. Crowds of students waited for their ship at every port. Great ceremonies acclaimed Dr. Sun and he made speech after speech. He had been ill and in pain for some time, but he had refused to give in to illness. Now he grew more ashen and weaker with every public appearance. Still he would not admit how sick he was. This was the moment of success—he was on his triumphant way to

Peking. Word came that in Canton General Chiang was turning into a successful military leader at the head of his
Whampoa cadets, wiping out one enemy stronghold after another.

At last General Chiang was doing what he had dreamed
about for years. At the head of an efficient military body, he
was taking his enemies by sheer courage and expertness. His
men were proud of themselves and he of them. At Waichow,
an ancient stronghold, which had not surrendered to any at-
tacker for centuries, he won a dramatic victory. Organized
peasants turned out to help him on his way, delighted with
troops that did not plunder as they went.

Just after this high moment, he received word that Dr. Sun
had died in Peking. A short time after Dr. Sun's death, General Chiang found that even before Dr. Sun had reached
Peking, he had discovered that the Revolutionary cause had
been betrayed. The unification that Peking proposed was another conservative scheme that would destroy the whole meaning of the Revolution and of the Nationalist Government. Perhaps that had hastened his death. At the end Dr. Sun had
commanded the men of his party to reject all proposals of the
northern group. What a bitter moment that must have been.

Where was the new Nationalist Government now? Their
leader was gone and they had been betrayed yet another time.
General Chiang had a growing private worry, too. The Russians had too much influence in his Whampoa Academy. They
sat in on government organizational meetings; they seemed to
be everywhere, helping to organize the peasants and the students. Dr. Sun had accepted Russian help and had not tried to
keep Communists out of the Nationalist offices. Chiang could
no longer do that. He made a decision and acted on it on his
own authority as Generalissimo of the Nationalist Army.

One night he seized all the Communists in the Canton Nationalist Party. He also took the men responsible for a strike
that had crippled Hong Kong shipping because he believed

that it was Communist-led. He ordered one of the Nationalist leaders close to him confined. He struck hard and bloodily but he believed that he had cleared out the Communists for once and for all. His friends and other leaders were astounded.

Now he was going to lead the Northern Expedition himself. He organized it carefully. It would move north in three prongs so as to wipe out all opposition and converge on Peking. By bribing them he won over some who stood in his way. This time the twelve-rayed sun of the Nationalist flag was going to fly over Peking.

The advance went brilliantly from Canton as far as Hankow. The local people cheered his troops along the way. At Hankow the advance paused. Nationalist leaders and Russian advisors quickly set up a government center. Hostile northern forces were gathering across the river from Nanking which Chiang could not afford to lose since it was to be his capital. He moved down river, ordered forces in one of the three prongs south of the river to push up toward Shanghai, and in sudden action took both important cities for himself. By this military maneuver he had left the Hankow group and separated his Nationalists from liberal influences of all kinds. He knew that wealthy friends of his in Shanghai would more than make up for the financial losses that he was incurring.

Some people claimed that he had betrayed the Nationalist, democratic cause. He paid no attention to this because he was not through yet. He started a thorough purge of all who had any connection with Chinese or Russian Communists. No one had dreamed that they would see the young general who had become Dr. Sun's right-hand man responsible for such a terrible event. Thousands of people in Shanghai were killed. Nanking waited anxiously for him to come and assume its leadership. He was the man at the top because military power was all that counted at this moment of China's history.

In the spring of 1927, instead of going to Nanking, General

Chiang left China and went to Japan. Nanking was safely his and perhaps, he thought, criticism would cool down after he left. His mind was on personal matters now. The Soong family was in Japan, too, and he was going to ask Mayling Soong to marry him. He was older than she, he could not speak English, and he had never been away from the Orient. Besides, he was not a Christian—but he was going to propose just the same. He would have to ask Mother Soong's permission to speak to Mayling. She had the reputation for being firm in her opinions and he had seen her enough to know that this reputation was justified.

When he reached Tokyo he found that the Soong family had left the city and gone to a resort. He followed, and at last, after being put off several times, he was able to make an appointment to call on Mother Soong.

Mother Soong had to admit to herself that General Chiang did not look as if he were much older than Mayling. He cut a rather dashing figure when he stood before her straight and slender with eyes that burned in a pale, chiseled face. But, he was not a Christian and that was why she was going to oppose the marriage. She and Charlie had been staunch Methodists for many years and their children had been brought up as Methodists, too. When she began to question him she broached every subject except religion. She would leave that to the last. When the moment came she was very direct.

"Are you willing to become a Christian like Mayling?" she said, looking at him hard through her spectacles.

"I am willing to study the Bible and learn about Christianity," he answered quietly. "When I have done that I shall decide whether or not I ought to join the church."

She was taken aback. Of course, he was right. If he had agreed to join the church just in order to marry Mayling, she would have questioned his sincerity. He had given the only right answer that was possible. She told him that he had her permission to ask Mayling to marry him.

Chiang had been afraid that the elderly woman would not be willing for her daughter to marry a soldier. He was surprised that the subject never came up, even indirectly. Had soldiering become respectable, he wondered. Had the fact that he had been educated in military schools helped? He did not know.

Chiang Kai-shek and Soong Mayling had known each other for five years. They were married in a Christian ceremony in the Soong Shanghai home at the end of December 1927, followed by an elegant combined Western and Oriental reception in a large hotel. All of General Chiang's friends and military men had to be invited and no expense was spared. In a special alcove was hung a large photograph of Dr. Sun, surrounded by flowers. The couple went to their beloved Hangchow for the honeymoon.

The Nationalist Government now centered in Nanking but Hankow continued to be the headquarters of the liberal, Russian-influenced group. At last they agreed to send the Russian advisors home but General Chiang knew that the Communists were still at work underground. They had a strong, undying conviction that no amount of bloodshed or suppression seemed to affect; it only grew stronger. During the next few years the Nationalist troops had orders to purge the Communists wherever they were found.

In 1932 some Chinese leaders joined with the Japanese and made the northwestern provinces into an independent state called Manchoukuo. However, General Chiang continued to believe that the Communists were his first and most dangerous enemy. The Chinese Communist Party had been formed in 1921 and had worked openly until his opposition drove it underground. Now he led one anti-Communist extermination campaign after another though he was warned that Japan planned a major invasion. And all extermination campaigns failed.

In 1933, General Chiang began his fifth attempt to rid China of the Communists and he felt sure it would be the last. This time he was going to use a new strategy. Hired German advisors worked with the Nationalist forces to encircle and blockade the main Communist center in Kiangsi Province. Highways were built which linked blockhouses around the area. When the time came, the Communists found themselves squeezed more and more tightly so that they could not get either food or arms. The end seemed to have come at last. Then, suddenly, the Nationalists found that most of the Reds, ninety thousand strong, had slipped out of their grasp and were miles away. In a slow, unnoticed process, local peasants exchanged their clothes for the uniforms of the Communists, a disguise that let the prisoners move out quietly through the blockade. The escaping forces were moving toward the northwest where they had friends.

A year later and six thousand miles away, one third of the original number of Communists reached their destination after enormous suffering. General Chiang's forces had followed, strafed, and harrassed them, but nothing, it seemed, could stop the Communists. He had failed again, but at least they were out of his way.

Just a year later the Japanese were pushing hard on China's northern borders again. A man called the Young Marshal, Chang Hsueh-liang, was under the greatest pressure. His men were Manchurian and they wanted to get home. The Young Marshal begged General Chiang to combine the Communists and Nationalist forces and oppose Japan for he believed that the situation was crucial. Chiang refused. In desperation the Young Marshal had General Chiang kidnapped and held in Sian on the promise that when he accepted eight proposed points, he would be released. The points included a commitment to join with the Communists to oppose Japan. The news of the kidnapping put Nanking into an uproar. People believed that General Chiang had already been killed and went into mass mourning. The military leader talked of bombing Sian. Madame Chiang begged him not to do so for he would destroy the General in an effort to save him. She, herself, flew to Sian.

General Chiang had been refusing to talk to anyone or to eat since he had been taken prisoner. When Madame Chiang arrived she got him to agree to the points, though not in writing, and succeeded in making the Young Marshal, who had always been their good friend, feel ashamed of himself. The Chiangs flew home for Christmas in 1936 taking the Young Marshal with them. What a celebration! The capital went wild.

This new development worried Japan for it meant that China's joint military power was ready to oppose her. She would have to plan her invasion carefully and act promptly. In 1937 Japan created an incident at Marco Polo Bridge near Peking. Her men on military manuvers claimed that they had been attacked by the Chinese. Japanese forces fanned out too readily; her planes strafed. Chiang Kai-shek and Mao Tse-tung, the leader of the Chinese Communists, joined without hesitation to resist the Japanese.

General Chiang now decided to act quickly, too. He ordered out his forces in an attack against the Japanese installations in Shanghai. Mayling could scarcely believe what she heard.

"You know that they cannot hold back the Japanese there," she said reprovingly. "Why waste so many good men?"

"It is not a waste," he said. "It will show the world that our soldiers are no longer afraid of fighting. It will attract the attention of the West to our plight."

"The Japanese will send their planes right over from Formosa. They will kill thousands of people in Shanghai, and you will be defeated." Mayling looked at her husband searchingly. Surely he did not love cruelty! It must be that the strategy of a military situation was so exciting that he forgot the people involved.

The attack on Shanghai ended in a bloody defeat but its heroes were praised and war songs memorialized them. Since Japan was advancing along the Shanghai-Nanking Railway to Nanking the capital city had to be moved. The government was first at Hankow, then further yet up the river, at Ichang, and at last at Chungking. Industries moved inland, and then the colleges. The people moved, too, in a long procession, in boats where there was water, on wheelbarrows, in sedan chairs, on horseback and on donkeys, but most of all on foot. It was one of the greatest migrations of history. Free China installed itself hundreds of miles inland. The fighting went on, the Communists always winning more battles against the Japanese than the Nationalists, and organizing the local people wherever they went.

Looking at the war from the safety of Chungking, General and Madame Chiang began to believe that their war was part of a world-wide struggle, that one day the Western powers would see that China was on the frontline of their battle, too. When Japan attacked Pearl Harbor in 1941, they believed that their idea had been proven. Now, surely, America would help China win the war in the Pacific. America had always been China's friend.

They were right. But the Americans who came to advise the Chinese insisted that the Nationalists and Communists must be closely allied against the Japanese. Instead, General Chiang still held back while Mao Tse-tung's forces won more and more popular support. The Communist leader had a network of organization among the peasants that made it possible for his men to check the Japanese with guerrilla tactics which the Nationalist forces with their organized battles could not begin to match.

When Japan was defeated in 1945 General Chiang was appointed to receive the surrender papers for China, but at that very time the Communists were already pouring into the areas the Japanese were vacating. America tried to stop them by airlifting in American and Nationalist forces and by sending the marines. General Chiang smiled to himself. Now, at last, the United States was taking the responsibility he thought she should have taken long ago. When he was advised on how to handle the restoration of Manchuria to China, he disagreed. Instead, he followed his own plan. He wanted it back for himself. He sent his men in and the Communists cut them off on the south. The situation was desperate.

The war was still not won. The temporary alliance of the Communists and the Nationalists fell apart. The war against the Communists still had to be fought. General and Madame Chiang went back to Nanking which was free of the Japanese at last, but no one seemed to have any heart to rebuild. The city had been ravaged by a terrible Japanese scourge. And now it seemed inevitable that the Reds were going to push the Nationalists on again. Still the National Congress met and General Chiang was elected President of the Nationalist Government of China. The Reds came on. The government moved and moved again. At last it was clinging to the very edge of the mainland at Canton. General Chiang prepared Formosa which was no longer Japan's as a place of refuge. In 1949 what was left of the Nationalist Government moved there. Mainland China was in the hands of the Chinese Communists with their capital at Peking.

Still General and Madame Chiang looked forward to a day when they would go back to the mainland in triumph. "We shall return," General Chiang said in his public speeches year after year. After all, the United States that had sent over so much help during the war against the Japanese was still sending the Nationalists help in Formosa. The island was becoming a display place of what could be done with intensified training and plenty of money. "If we had only had longer!" Generalissimo Chiang Kai-shek sometimes said to Mayling. "Twenty years was not enough time to win against both the Japanese and the Communists."

10

1898–
James Yen

ORIGINATOR OF THE THOUSAND
CHARACTER MOVEMENT

"I don't know how to write a letter to my family at home and if they send me one written by a letter-writer, I can't read it to see how they are!" a Chinese laborer in France said one day during the First World War. He drew a deep sigh and dropped his head onto his arms folded across his knees as he sat disconsolately on the ground.

"I'll write a letter for you," a young Chinese man in a Western-style suit said cheerfully. "Tell me what you want to say." He leaned down to listen to the laborer and wrote quickly in his notebook. The younger man was tall and slender and lively in his manner. He gave the impression of being full of ideas and ready for anything. The laborer turned and looked at him while he wrote, his face beginning to lighten.

"Let me guess where you come from," he said. "Your dialect is from the western parts—right? Perhaps Szechuan?"

"You guessed it," the other answered. "Szechuan is my old home."

China had entered World War I in 1917 by providing labor

battalions. Thousands of her men were here in France, isolated from their families. They were isolated by more than distance because almost all them were illiterate. They could neither write home nor read the stylized letters their families sometimes had written by a public scribe.

The young Chinese man who was taking the letter for the laborer was Y. C. James Yen who had accompanied the men to France as one of their interpreters. He belonged to an old and scholarly family. His father was an aristocrat who saw that it was the fashion to educate one's sons in European as well as Chinese learning so he sent James to America to study and he became a graduate of Yale University.

When he was growing up, James Yen had never paid much attention to laborers or *coolies*. As a member of a scholarly family one ordered them around, treated them decently, and then forgot about them. But now, in France, his job was with laborers and he watched them with a sudden, new interest. They worked hard—much harder than anyone else. They were shrewd and resourceful. They were full of hearty humor. They spent practically nothing on themselves and saved up their pay to take or send home. But, they had no way of communicating with their families.

What could be done about it? The Chinese written language was made up of hundreds of complicated characters that simply had to be memorized. There was no such thing as a logical alphabet or system of phonetics. Laborers like these had never had a chance to go to school. Even if they had, the kind of lives they lived would not give them time to keep them in practice enough for writing.

Every day James Yen went around and chatted with the men. He made it part of his work to keep them feeling that someone was interested in them. Many of them loved to tell jokes and when they did the whole group of them in any one place would shout out in good-natured laughter. James had to admit that with all his education he sometimes missed a fine point in what the men were saying because he did not know *their* language well enough. He appreciated the down-to-earth quality of the men more and more. He gradually began to grow proud of them as his countrymen. It was easy to visualize the great spread of the Chinese countryside dotted with villages and hamlets where people like these lived, generation after generation.

But many a time he came across a man who was lonely and worried because he had no news from home. The Chinese people had always cherished their family connections and here were thousands of Chinese who were not able to continue those connections since they could not read and write. On the day that James Yen wrote the letter for the disconsolate man sitting on the ground with his head on his arms, he got an idea.

Why not organize the men into small groups and teach them to read in long evenings when they had nowhere to go? Although they were highly intelligent human beings, they were still illiterate in the twentieth century!

It was easy enough to say that he would teach the men to read and write but how on earth could he do it? It took years to learn the Chinese written form. Chinese was much harder to write than English for the usual vocabulary was made up of about five thousand characters, or words. Well, he decided, he would reduce the number of characters. He would make up a word list of the words he actually heard the men use.

Then he began to sift out even the shortened vocabulary list. Every word that was not absolutely necessary was dropped. He got the list down to three thousand but even that was still too many to remember. He cut it lower and lower. At last it reached one thousand.

What could he do now with one thousand Chinese characters? He pretended to himself that there were no more and began to prepare lessons that used no other words. To his own astonishment he found that it was perfectly possible. The thousand-character word list worked!

The other interpreters had been watching what James Yen was doing. Now he asked them to help organize the men into groups. When the day was over the lessons began. At first the men handled the rough sheets which had a few large characters on them with embarrassed unfamiliarity. They were not supposed to be students, they were laborers! They peered at the blackboard where a teacher was writing a word, and then looked back at their sheets. One stroke this way, one stroke that, and a little square in the middle. Yes, that word on the blackboard was the same as this one on their lesson sheets. Some of them laughed like delighted children when they saw the similarity.

James Yen was getting excited now. He went on with his plans enthusiastically. He was beginning to dream all sorts of dreams for he had suddenly realized that after they had taught the men how to read they would have nothing but their lesson sheets to read! Everything that was published in Chinese used many characters besides his One Thousand. There was nothing to do but to start a newspaper that did not go beyond his vocabulary. He went to Paris and worked out a plan with a printer.

When the first issue of the one-page newspaper came out and arrived at the place where the men were working, he watched them. They were so absorbed that they did not even see him strolling around among them. At last one of them caught sight of him. He leaped up and came hurrying toward him, the newssheet fluttering in his hand.

"Teacher," he said, his eyes shining, "I know I can read the lessons, but listen while I read even *printed* words!" His finger moved down the page while he read an item of local news aloud. Then he looked at James Yen in sheer delight.

"Of course," James Yen said. "You are now an educated man." The fellow guffawed and would have turned away, but James Yen stopped him. "What I am saying is really true," he said. "From now on you can add more and more words to the ones you know. You have entered a new world. Now your eyes can see where before they were blind."

"It is true, it is true," the laborer said, suddenly serious. Then his face lit again. "When I go home I'll teach my Inside One [my wife]! Wait until she sees what I have learned to do!" He bounded away, a bronzed, sinewy, enthusiastic young man.

The newspaper James Yen had begun to have published in Paris was called *The Chinese Laborers' Weekly*. It sold for one centime. Some of the men were so afraid it would go out of print because there would not be enough money to keep it going that they gave some of their savings to James Yen to make sure it would continue.

James Yen moved out further into his dream. He could see that this system of education which used a limited, workable vocabulary, something like basic English, could be put to work much more widely than just among Chinese labor battalions in France. He began to think through plans for an expanded application of the system. Why not try it out in rural areas back at home in China? Why not even plan a mass education movement?

It would take testing in an experimental center, it would take careful planning, and it would need money even though it must be kept as simple and down-to-earth as possible. First he and his friends needed to choose a spot for a demonstration. The plan would have to be "sold" to the entire population. The country people would not be as eager to learn as the young men who wanted to write home. Leaders in rural communities did not change easily. He thought about the plan more and more and tried to keep its main objectives in mind so that they would not be buried under the necessary details.

James Yen realized that he was not the only originator of simplified Chinese. At this very time, a Chinese professor in Peking University, Dr. Hu Shih, had launched a movement called the Literary Revolution in colleges and universities. He wanted to do away with the stiff, formal classical written forms which had to be learned as a special language and to encourage publishers instead to use the colorful everyday way of speaking. If this were done, people could understand what they read for it would be published in the language they spoke. Modern Chinese literature would be set free.

Publishers responded to Dr. Hu Shih's ideas very quickly. New magazines, especially magazines for young people, appeared one after another. The change had an enormous effect on Chinese students. They thought it heralded a new day. New ideas swept the country, spread by the press. Everywhere the young people began to demand that their country modernize. Dr. Hu Shih had certainly succeeded in beginning a literary revolution which would also contribute to the broader political revolution that was going on under the leadership of Dr. Sun Yat-sen, the founder of the Nationalist Chinese Government.

But James Yen was not thinking of students or of politics. Laborers were not going to be able to read even Dr. Hu Shih's everyday style. It had far too many words. He was determined not to let himself be swept away from his goal. He confined all his plans rigidly to the magic One Thousand.

Before he left France to return to China at the end of the war, James Yen knew that he had found the cause he wanted to give himself to. He was what was called an intellectual, but he could never be just a scholar again. He would not be able to forget the laborers and shut himself away in any ivory tower with ancient literature, no matter how beautiful. Even the Ancients had said "People are the foundation of a nation. If the foundation is firm, then the nation will enjoy tranquility."

When he reached China and once again saw the thousands who had never dreamed of knowing how to read and write, his plans began to expand. Was there not some way to spread the Thousand Character method across the whole extent of China? He began to believe firmly that there was. Of course, the people's leaders were going to have to be won over first. James Yen and a few of the young men who had seen what had happened in France, began to work. They talked to the community leaders in villages or towns, the town counsellors. They held socials and group meetings. In towns the schools were drawn in almost at once. Students began to volunteer to be teachers in what were soon known as Thousand Character Schools. The students went from house to house recruiting their own pupils.

In Wuhan, the triple city of Wuchang, Hanyang, and Hankow, James Yen and his men, or The Team, got a wonderful response. A great meeting was held at Central China University and the Mass Education Association was formed.

This development was very dramatic, but as time passed James Yen saw that the more truly dramatic development was going on in the villages. It started when he or one of his team went to call on the Village Elder.

"Sir, can you tell us how many people in your village read?" he would ask.

"Oh, I don't know. We have never asked them such a question," the man said, standing in his doorway and inviting them in with a bow and a motion of his hand. "Please, come in and have tea. I don't dare, Teachers—" He did not finish the polite sentence.

The young men went in, and after proper refusals, at last were seated in the formal guestroom of the house. A small boy came running with a pot of tea and cups.

"Would you not like to know how many can read?" James Yen pressed.

"It does not matter. It is not important. A farmer does not have to read. Tradition has it that a man who works with his hands is illiterate."

"Oh, Sir, but in these times your village would be much richer and stronger if your people knew the characters."

"How can they know the characters? They are grown men and they have no time to be students."

James Yen told the Village Elder what had happened in France; what had taken place in Wuhan. Then he said, "Wouldn't you like to start such a school here in your village? It would be in the evening after work and it would not cost you anything."

Another round of tea was poured and drunk before the talk was over. But the plan had been laid. The school could use the village temple, for no Chinese god would be against learning. The night to begin was set.

On that night, the Village Elder himself told the people about the new school. He promised that if they spent an hour every evening studying, in four months they would be able to read the Thousand Character Book which he held up for all to see.

That was the way it went in village after village. On the great evening when the school began, the crowd always laughed and applauded. Old and young were mixed together, even a few women were usually standing inconspicuously on the outskirts of the crowd. How jolly and good-natured they were, James Yen thought over and over with growing pride.

Any people in a village who could read were urged to become teachers in the new school or schools. A spirit of excited expectancy swept over one dull little hamlet after another. The schools progressed and the people seemed awakened from a long sleep. James Yen was providing ability at the grass roots, preparing the masses for intelligent citizenship.

In the meantime the Mass Education Association begun in

Wuhan became a nationwide organization with prominent men on its board. Dr. Sun Yat-sen, as the founder of the new Nationalist Government, was trying to get supporters for it. But Dr. Sun seemed not to realize its full significance. In Shanghai he was busy writing about his political theories in his own dry, long-winded style. He knew of Dr. Hu Shih's work but he did not seem to understand that there might be a connection between the peasants who were learning to read, the students who were revolting against the old ways, and the democratic government he hoped to establish. Still, he had gone around the world several times to enlist overseas Chinese in his cause. By now he was discouraged; perhaps that was the trouble.

Generalissimo Chiang Kai-shek, the military leader of the Nationalist Government, endorsed James Yen's work. Madame Chiang was enthusiastic and perhaps she influenced him. He gave as full support as he could when the government was unstable. James Yen carefully did not let himself become involved with the government. He wanted to help the people as a whole, whatever their political views.

After three or four years of experimenting, James Yen and his team chose a spot where they would make a real demonstration. It was clear to them now that they were going to do more than teach people to read and write. There were 1900 counties, or *hsien*, in all China. A county was the real community unit. They chose one called Tinghsien or Ting County. One reason they chose it was that it had an old civil service examination hall in the county seat, just the place for their headquarters and for large meetings.

James Yen and his team did not take their own families to Tinghsien right away. They lived in a broken-down temple and spent most of their time getting acquainted with the people in the county's villages. Some of the team had lived abroad and held high degrees from foreign universities, but they kept that to themselves for it would separate them from the villagers if it were known. These men could have been university professors if they chose, but they had chosen rather to come to Tinghsien.

Some of the team did give up and go home because they could not adjust to the life. Those who stayed had to adapt their lives so that they saw themselves from the villagers' point of view. One of the team might improve cabbages, another cotton, another breed a better kind of hogs, yet another cross breeds of chickens so that the hens laid more eggs. Gradually they were able to introduce simple changes in the way farmhouses were built by suggesting more holes in the mud walls for windows—but there could not be too many because of the cold. The staff had to remember all the time that they had to stay within the old village society and yet manage to create a new one. They were researchers who worked with people and things in their tests rather than theories and cold statistics.

After a time, in village after village, the Thousand Character classes were gathering in many a courtyard or on someone's threshing floor for the evening's work. In winter they used a temple or a guild hall. The graduates became teachers. Even pupils who had not finished the course often taught others in what they called the Pupil-Teacher Plan. For the first time a farmer could call himself a scholar and it changed him by giving him a new self-confidence and self-respect.

As time passed graduates formed themselves into a Fellow-Scholar Association. Age had nothing to do with membership. Old and young, men and some women belonged, though the older women were very hard to convince that they could have anything to do with books because they had been told for so long that they could not learn anything from them.

One of the interesting things the Fellow-Scholar Association did was to start the practice of writing the main news of the day in chalk on a public wall that had been painted black.

Until there was a newspaper printed in the Thousand Character vocabulary the Wall News provided thumbnail information of great interest. A few farmers would often stand rapt before the wall, sounding the words to themselves.

By the time radio broadcasts were possible, the Tinghsien Fellow-Scholars were working in 472 villages. Not all of these could afford a radio. The Fellow-Scholar Association set up a program which broadcast at a certain time of day. The villagers gathered then at the point closest to them to listen. It seemed a miracle.

James Yen and his men used still another way of teaching. They developed the old Chinese idea of traveling actors who presented plays that were historical, merely amusing, or propaganda for the Mass Education Movement. The Fellow-Scholar Association worked out plots that showed the dangers of opium smoking, the value of better roads, and most of all of learning to read. They also stressed the importance of health. The plays, the radio, and the Wall Papers all tried to make people understand some things they could do to check epidemics and to save lives by cleanliness.

At last, a weekly Thousand Character newspaper, *The Farmer*, began. It seemed to combine all the values of the other methods because one could go back and reread and think over what had been said. Besides, it was a printed sheet to hold in the hand or to keep on the table under the ancestral scrolls.

Often at night when the long days were done, the team talked things over. "We have a lion by the tail. He is dragging us. We can't limit what we have undertaken," someone would say almost groaning. Another would not say anything, engrossed in taking off straw sandals and putting his sore feet into a small wooden tub of warm water. "They want to know everything, to try everything," another said half-laughing.

"Who ever said the Chinese farmer was satisfied with his life and never wanted to change!"

"Remember that what we are doing in Tinghsien is only a sample. We hope it will be used in many places," James Yen told them. Somehow, no matter how hard a day he put in, he never lost his fresh look or his buoyancy.

"If the government ever settles down, perhaps it will use our sample," someone said and then drank deeply from his cup of steaming tea.

"For now, let's go on trying the plan out in different parts of the country," James Yen said quickly. "This is in the north. We will try one west and south. Don't let's worry about the government. It is most important of all to stay free." He spoke with feeling.

There was no end to the possibilities of a new language that almost everyone could learn. After the textbooks and the newspapers and the plays, there was the need for a whole new literature. A Department of People's Literature was set up. Old stories were rewritten and biographies of important people, information about other countries, science—all were put into the Thousand Character vocabulary. When the books came out in the usual Chinese format of soft-backed paper books, they were taken to the villages in traveling libraries. After a while the library contained a thousand volumes. Books were so inexpensive that even a farmer could buy his own.

When the work in Tinghsien was begun around 1924, 80,000 out of the total of 400,000 people were of an age and an ability to be educated. In 1936 most of the 80,000 were full of enthusiasm about what they could do, and eager to help. The whole program was a volunteer program. The experiment had proven itself even though constant adaptation was needed. People had learned to work together, they had learned to care for the whole community and not just their own families. They wanted to govern themselves locally. This idea of local self-government was one of the things that Dr. Sun Yat-sen had had in mind, too. The three experimental centers—north, west and south—tried it out successfully. It spread over other parts of China. The Nationalist Government at last authorized its being established in every single province. Farmers were making almost twice what they were before the plan began. Everything was favorable—except war with Japan arose.

After the program had been in progress for twenty years, James Yen told a friend in America that they now felt sure that in ten years' time it could wipe out illiteracy and double the farmer's income. He went on to say that the farmer's life had been improved in many ways—in education, in earning, in self-government and in health. The plan was one that could prepare China to become a great modern nation.

James Yen and his staff had trained five thousand higher officers and thirty thousand village heads how to teach the people, when China had to move her capital inland to Chungking because of the war with Japan. In 1940 the National College of Rural Reconstruction was begun near that city to train men to work with country people. Generalissimo Chiang Kai-shek approved it and supported it in every way, and every one of the provincial governments of Free China sent donations to help finance it. Not even the war could stop the Thousand Character, or Mass Education Movement.

But the war was a world war. The Allies were involved in the Pacific. The United States poured in her men and guns. James Yen sadly reflected that the money which it took to finance five hours of the war would be sufficient to teach forty-seven million people in China to read. He wondered when the leaders of the world would come to realize that nothing can succeed unless it serves the people, for people are a nation's greatest asset.

11

1893–

Mao Tse-tung

LEADER OF THE
CHINESE COMMUNIST REVOLUTION

In 1907 a boy named Mao Tse-tung set out for high school in a town fifteen miles up the Hsiang River from his home village, Shao Shan, in Hunan Province. Shao Shan had no such school and he was eager to get more education. His baggage was made up of two parcels which he carried on either end of a pole slung over his shoulder and contained only some articles of worn clothing and a few precious books. He was not running away from home although his father, a rice merchant, was a bad-tempered, bitter-tongued man who had strongly disagreed with his plans for more schooling and had given him only enough money for his tuition, none for his food and lodging.

But the fourteen-year-old boy did not care about that. He would manage somehow for he was "bitten" by books. From the time he had learned to read in the village school, he had read everything he could find. His teacher was delighted with him and loaned him all the books he had. Soon Mao discovered the tale of a band of adventurous robbers called *All Men Are Brothers*. He devoured its endless pages not only once but over and over. It came to be a secret source of ideas and dreams, even of inspiration.

In high school he had to study the ancient classics, but he still read everything else he could. He never knew what time of night it was and often read until morning. He made friends with a boy named Hsiao San who soon became not only his friend but his admiring follower. Hsiao San found a book called *Great Heroes of the World* which had been translated into Chinese from an American edition. Mao could not lay it down until he had finished it. He was surprised by the story of George Washington which it contained and he told Hsaio San that there was a lesson to be learned from it. China, like America, could grow rich and strong if she were free.

Hsiao San stared at his friend. What was he saying? He seemed to be making an announcement, stating a decision. But Mao gazed off into the distance unaware of his friend. "We need great people like these," he added finishing what he had said before. Hsiao San was always to remember that moment. Years later he would think back and realize that it had been a fateful one.

There were good reasons why Mao should be so strongly affected by this book. Two events involving his own village had already torn down the wall between him and the outer world. When he was eleven a terrible famine had caused desperate peasants to attack the magistrate's offices in Changsha, the provincial capital, demanding that rice graineries be opened to save the starving people. Instead, the peasants were punished and their leaders were executed. The insurrection had been a failure but the boy Mao was close to the whole affair. He saw men from his own area lose their lives only because they demanded food from hoarded stores. The school boys had talked the whole thing over excitedly and some had shouted at him, "Your father is a rice merchant! What have you to say?" What did he have to say for after all rice was the only security his family had.

The second event that shook him was another insurrection. Members of an old secret society which had been organized to protect peasants from unfair landlords tried to attack such landlords in the Shao Shan area. They were caught and punished. Their leaders were executed in an open field where everyone could scarcely avoid seeing what took place. Mao was thirteen by this time. He heard all the reports of the event; he saw the bodies of men, some of whom he had known.

Twice before he went away to school, then, he had seen rebellions and both times they had been intended only to get justice for the ordinary people. No wonder the story of George Washington excited him.

Still, Mao and his friend Hsiao San had to admit that it looked as though China's Manchu government in Peking was ready to make reforms. Once the old Manchu empress dowager was no longer in power, things would surely change. Two outstanding reformers had a program ready to go into effect and the young emperor was enthusiastically supporting it, too. The boys watched the news and waited for the new day to come. But there was one worry—none of the reforms seemed to take peasants into account. Everything seemed to be for others.

When holidays came, Mao and Hsiao San wandered over the Hunan countryside. They talked with ruddy-faced farmers and often listened to arguments between the Hunanese who are famous for their hot tempers. They also are famous for quick courage and daring and often the boys heard tales that seemed something like events in *All Men Are Brothers*. Mao and his friend felt free and adventurous. They went bare-backed until they were burned to a dark brown like the peasants they met.

"Don't you see," Mao sometimes said to his friend, "these

are the *real* people. They are polite to us and loyal to each other. People in cities and towns are not like that. They don't care what happens to anyone else. I know because I found that to be true, until you became my friend."

The two boys trudged over the curious broken hills among ancient temples and pagodas or between rice paddies as they followed the course of the winding Hsiang River. They went as far as Changsha thirty miles from school. There they saw the Junior College and discussed whether they should try to enter it after they had finished high school.

"What ought I to do?" Mao asked his friend. "The peasants need everything—and perhaps I ought to work for them. But how I love my books!"

Hsiao San knew that Mao did not want an answer from him, but from himself. He waited.

"I could enter the Junior College and become a teacher of peasants," Mao continued uncertainly. His eyes rested on Hsiao San, but he did not really see him. A phrase from the writings of Confucius was going through his mind, and then a dramatic, brave episode from his favorite book followed quickly. He smiled suddenly.

In 1911 the two boys were accepted at the Junior College in Changsha. It was early spring. Almost before they had time to settle into the term's work, rebellion burst into their lives again. Hwang Hsing, a follower of the famous revolutionary leader Sun Yat-sen, was trying for the fourth time to seize the seat of government in the capital. This government was part of the Manchu empire system which Dr. Sun hoped to overthrow and replace with a Chinese republic. Mao had heard of Sun Yat-sen and knew of other attempts to seize the magistrate's office. The story of this attempt came out gradually. Students gathered in excited knots, the two boys among them.

"Hwang Hsing had thirty of Dr. Sun's party men [Kuomintang] with him and eight hundred others with arms," one man said.

"Then how could they fail so miserably?" another demanded.

"The armed men did not arrive on time. Hwang Hsing and his handful of men arrived first and had no support. The timing was all off."

"Forty-three of the best men were cut down," another student put in.

"And twenty-seven were captured," still another said.

"What happened to them?" Mao demanded, and suddenly all eyes turned on him because of something in his voice.

"They and two more were executed."

The Seventy-two Martyrs soon became famous all over China. Mao and Hsiao San began to doubt that people were going to wait for the reformers. They heard more and more talk of rebellion. The young emperor as well as the empress dowager had died late in 1908, and a baby had been put on the throne. The regent who acted for him was hopelessly conservative.

Mao brooded over his country's situation all through the summer holiday. He began to read about politics and when he went back to school he wrote articles on the subject (signed with a fictitious name) and posted them on the bulletin board. He cut off his queue and went out with other boys on what they called "queue-chopping expeditions" until he had accumulated ten of them. These expeditions came to be a kind of sport.

He was really waiting to see what was going to happen. Surely there was going to be a great rebellion and Peking would be freed from the Manchus! But when the Revolution came, it came by accident. On October 10, 1911, a bomb exploded where munitions were being prepared secretly in Hankow. The Revolution had to be up-dated. Mao, now a young man of eighteen, went to Hankow to join the Revolutionary Army. Soon it would be marching on Peking. But he was only an ordinary soldier assigned to garrison duty, which meant being a servant to young officers. It was a disillusioning, miserable experience. The soldiers talked about nothing but violence. Discipline was brutal. Men lost their heads for small offences, for execution seemed to be the common punishment.

Worst of all, Mao believed that the Revolution was failing for Dr. Sun now agreed to let Yuan Shih-k'ai, a reactionary warlord in the north, take his place as President of the new Nationalist Government which had been set up. Mao grew depressed and left the army. He lived in a poor boarding house and worried over the state of his country. He looked at advertisements for job openings and even applied for one or two. Then suddenly he knew that what he wanted was to study again. He and Hsiao San applied to the Teacher Training College in Changsha for admittance. They were there for six years.

These were important years for Mao because in them he found a teacher who was interested in helping him to write well, and because in them he discovered the public library. He did a great deal of reading on socialism. He was still so addicted to reading that he often read all night and went around in a daze of sleepy-eyed half attention the next day. By now he was tall and heavy set, with hulking shoulders. He moved in a massive way. Those around him tended to hold back a little from him, perhaps because he was already showing signs of becoming a leader.

Mao read about the Kuomintang or the Nationalist Party and he also read the writings of the reformers from whom he had expected so much. In 1914 he decided to form a student organization of his own. He called it New Peoples Study Organization. Its charter members were eleven students from the normal school.

China entered the World War I in 1917. She was to send labor battalions to work behind the lines. Some Hunanese volunteered to go and Mao's New Peoples Study Organization provided the cost of their travel to the coast. Students were going, too, for they were anxious to go abroad and learn something about Europe. A plan was worked out whereby students could both work and study in France. Mao was put in charge enroute of the group going from Hunan to Peking.

"I've no real wish to go abroad now," he confessed to Hsiao San, "but I want to see Peking and to learn French and English—and, perhaps, I'll do some writing."

Hsiao San smiled. "You and your books! One minute I think you are a politician and an organizer, perhaps even a military strategist—the next you have disappeared in a forest of books." (The Chinese word for library really is "forest of books.")

Mao helped the students go through their training period in Peking and saw them off, and then he went to Peking University. He had dreamed of getting there some day and now here he was. The university was the scholarly center of China. He had a friend there, a teacher who had praised his work at the Teacher Training College in Changsha saying, "Follow the example of Mao Tse-tung who writes elegantly and honestly." Now he hurried to look him up because he had to have some kind of a job to support himself. His friend found him one in the university library, but it was a small, menial job and in many ways it was disappointing. He could not be himself, for he only carried books here and there, and the hours were very long. He was beginning to write poetry, but he had no time for it now.

Mao was terribly poor. His student's gown was worn threadbare. He began to read about anarchist leaders. He dreamed of being one himself and of leading such a group. But when the northern winter came, Peking was so beautiful that he was spellbound. Twenty years after this time he spoke of the winter plum blossoms opening over an ice-bound lake, of winter-jewelled trees. He was twenty-five now and as he matured he seemed to have two clear sides to his nature—he was bookworm and poet, but he was also a clear-thinking, ruthless maker of strategy.

He fell in love with the daughter of his old Changsha professor and perhaps for this reason he began to have more contacts in the life of the university. He enjoyed the social gatherings, the scholarly discussions. Had he been wrong in thinking seriously about anarchy and socialism, he sometimes wondered? He did not know Dr. Hu Shih, a famous professor, personally, but he was a man who had been in America and returned to propose a new Chinese writing style using the everyday language of the people. It was a dramatic break with the tradition of the past and Mao heartily approved it.

Still another professor, Ch'en Tu-hsiu, who edited a magazine called *New Youth* influenced Mao even more. Ch'en's ideas were as startling as his dramatic style. He attracted students like a magnet. The university was uneasy about him yet it had no real reason to dismiss him.

All winter Mao kept his 7 A.M. to 9 P.M. job in the library. Whenever he had a free moment he wandered over the city, walking on the city wall, gazing at the magnificent buildings of the past, and courting his sweetheart. When a group of students were ready to go to France he started with them toward Shanghai, accompanying them as far as the northern seaport of Tientsin where they embarked. He was penniless and had to borrow from a friend to get to Shanghai even by walking. He was very thin now, and his hair hung to his shoulders. His clothing was threadbare. Yet he had seen Peking. He had filled himself with its beauty and he had gulped down all the reading he could in the university library. For a whole winter he had not thought about politics.

Now he was a wandering scholar and he took in all the

sights on his way south. He visited the tomb of Confucius and the famous sacred mountain T'ai Shan where emperors of the past had made sacrifices to Heaven. All the wonderful things of his country's history became more real because of that journey. As if to climax it all, when he reached Shanghai he borrowed a little money again and there he married the girl he had been courting in Peking.

Back at last in his own province, Hunan, he found everything in upheaval. While he had been away, the Peking government had sent in an expedition to stop a rebellion. Mao threw himself into action because the men holding the positions of governor and military inspector were worthless. He began a magazine called *Hsiang River Monthly Review* which he filled with propaganda, and began to lay his plans. He organized a student strike and decided to use the New Peoples Study Organization to oppose the government. Suddenly he realized that this was just the kind of thing Professor Ch'en at Peking University would approve of, the man who was so liberal and free in his style. He hurried to Peking with the Organization paying his way. Professor Ch'en encouraged and approved of revolt but Mao found that he was vague as to how to carry it out. Mao rushed back to Changsha. He would have to make his own plans.

The next May fourth, 1919, events exploded in Peking. Word came that the peacemakers in Versailles, meeting after the end of World War I, had given Japan the territory in north China that had formerly been in German hands. The Chinese people already had strong feelings against Japan because of the Sino-Japanese War of 1895 and because of demands for concessions that Japan had made from time to time. Now furious protest broke out. Mao's Professor Ch'en had plans ready. He called a mass meeting of students and told them how to organize. A great strike began in Peking. Everything stopped—trains discontinued their service, shops closed, workers did not report. The strike spread to Shanghai, to Nanking, and then to Hankow. China had never seen such a thing as this—and led by students!

The May Fourth Incident which soon became the May Fourth Movement showed students what they could do. Mao listened to the reports, read what was available in the press and thought it all over. This was an urban movement, not a peasant one. It was influenced by Communist teachings. A special edition of *New Youth,* Professor Ch'en's publication, carried an article about Marxism. More and more translations of Marx and Lenin came into print. Some voices called on the whole Orient to rise against the colonial countries that had invaded the Far East with trade and with religious propaganda.

Mao was very much excited about what was happening. He strengthened his New Peoples Study Organization and made it into what amounted to a revolutionary secret society. "All this talk of democracy and of getting anything changed without a strong army is a mistake," he told the closest members of the society. "The strikes have shown us that we will have to use mass action." Those who listened agreed. "We will have to form a Communist Party of our own," he continued. "We will choose just a few to begin it." He did not look in anyone's direction, but each one present asked himself, "Will I be one?"

The First Congress of the Chinese Communist Party met in Shanghai at the end of June 1921. Twelve carefully chosen persons were present. Mao was there and so were his Professor Ch'en and the head of the Peking University library, both of whom had by now resigned from their positions. The two professors took the lead in planning the conference.

Such a meeting had to be held secretly because not only the Peking government but the Nationalist Party, or Kuomintang, would be watching. So far the Kuomintang permitted Party members to be Communists, but the organization of a Chinese

Communist Party was another matter. The Congress began in a quiet girls' school in the French Concession. Concessions were guarded by police of their own nationality, and the school was closed for the summer holiday. The Congress hired its own cook and guards to watch out for anyone who might unexpectedly interrupt. The meeting was to last for seven days, but on the fourth a man rushed in past the guards asking for a Mr. Wang who was chairman of another organization.

"That organization is not here but just down the street," one of the young Communists told him. The moment the intruder had left, the Communist member said, "I suspect there is no such man as Mr. Wang. That fellow is a spy!"

"Send someone over to the place he said he was looking for," another man said quickly. "Check on him."

In a few minutes the messenger hurried back. "No chairman of that name! The fellow never even went there!"

The meeting broke up. Most of the delegates left hastily. Ten minutes later a dozen policemen were on the spot. All they could find was some Marxist literature, and persons living in the French Concession were allowed to have that. The police had no justifiable reasons to make any arrests.

The Communist Congress first thought of moving to Hangchow but many people would be there during the summer holiday and so they settled on a smaller place where they hired a boat and bought food. A light mist gathered over the water and shrouded them while they met all day. The most important decision they made was to stay with the Kuomintang until they could find a satisfactory way to take decisive action, but the Congress also set up a framework for its own organization.

Mao did not know it but at the very time when he and the other Congress members were organizing the Chinese Communist Party, another Chinese named Chu Teh with whom he would later fight against the Nationalists, was gathering a group of Chinese students together in Germany where he was studying, to pledge themselves to making China into a Communist state. Chu Teh was a keen, well-educated man who knew much more about Western history than Mao. On separate sides of the world they were moving toward the same dramatic event.

When the Kuomintang held its first national congress in Canton where it centered, early in 1924, Mao attended it. He met General Chiang Kai-shek for the first time. Chiang had just been in Russia studying Russian military methods and he had been much impressed. Mao also met Dr. Sun Yat-sen. During the meeting Communist members of the Kuomintang urged that some of them be on the Nationalist Central Executive Committee. Mao's name was put up by a man named Hu Han-min. Now Mao found himself at the center of both the Communist and the Nationalist organizations. He was not a great speaker but people soon discovered that he was most useful as a contact man, and as a lobbyist.

Hu Han-min, who had put up Mao's name, was one of the Nationalist "Big Three" along with General Chiang Kai-shek and a man named Wang Ching-wei. Hu was an elderly man whose position was second only to that of Dr. Sun himself at this time. Now Hu asked Mao to serve as his secretary. Mao realized that his powers would be enormous for Hu was aging. Mao was soon acting for him in all sorts of ways. Official papers and many sources of information lay open to him. Decisions waited for him. Hu was glad to rely on this smart young peasant, for he, too, was of peasant origin.

The next few months were like a strange dream, wonderful but frightening. Mao found that he had to play one Party against the other, carry secret messages for both, and travel back and forth between Canton and Shanghai many times. When it seemed that Peking and Canton were at last about to be unified under the Nationalist government, Dr. Sun started north for the great event. He died of cancer before the unification took place, but not before he discovered that he had been deceived. Chaos followed his death and Mao fell ill from strain. He went home to Hunan leaving his Communist Party responsibilities to a brother who was in Shanghai.

While Mao lay ill, he rethought everything. Years ago he had believed that the peasants were China's strength and hope. Now he came back to this conviction. When he recovered in the spring he went all over the province organizing the peasants. The warlords and the landlords soon discovered what he was about and put a price on his head. He was thinner than ever now, tall, and burned brown by the sun. He looked like a tax collector or a teacher. He had to use an assumed name and travel at night. His anger against the well-off farmers, the middle class, burned hot. "Now all my past comes together to make my future," he wrote to himself. "I began with the peasants and I have come back to them. They are the foundation of a nation." That sounded familiar. Was he not quoting Confucius? He had to laugh at himself.

Things became so dangerous for him that at last he escaped to Canton where not many people knew what he had been doing. There he was astonished at the way things had changed. "Hu Han-min has been sent to Moscow! Chiang Kai-shek is striding about in his fine uniform as head of the new Whampoa Military Academy. Wang Ching-wei is boss now that Dr. Sun is dead," a Communist friend told him. "Watch your step!" he warned. The coalition of Peking and Canton had never come about.

Wang Ching-wei remembered Mao as Hu Han-min's secretary. He engaged Mao to do a few jobs. He edited a small secret publication, he gave some lectures at the Whampoa Academy, he was spokesman for the Communist Party.

In the secret darkness of an evening spent in a Communist friend's house, Mao shook his massive head in mystification.

"How can Heaven ask me to act as a Kuomintang and believe as a Communist! I am trusted by both sides when I am a collaborator! I am dedicated to peasant revolution, but the Kuomintang is promising them just enough in the way of reforms for General Chiang to get their cooperation while he tries to march on Peking!" He raised his head and looked at his friend. "You know as well as I do that Chiang is against revolutionary peasant uprisings. He will use the peasants for his own purposes, but that is all."

"True, true," the other said. The silence that fell over them seemed ominous, as though both were seeing something sinister in the future.

The number of Communist members in the Kuomintang increased. Mao pushed forward, too. He organized the peasants in the provinces where Chiang's expedition to Peking would pass. When the expedition to the north began, Mao was back in his own home province getting the peasants ready to collaborate with Chiang's Revolutionary or Nationalist army. For now, it was the only thing to do. The army marched along the Hsiang River supported by the peasants in every way. Then it turned eastward toward Shanghai and soon the Canton Nationalist Government moved to Hankow in its wake.

Suddenly a shattering blow fell. When Chiang Kai-shek reached Shanghai in March, 1927, he first cut off his relations with the Kuomintang in Hankow. Next he began a bloody purge of Communists in Shanghai which he soon extended to the whole country. The people who had been so loyal to him recoiled in disbelief.

Mao had laid a foundation for peasant organization in the work he had been doing in Hunan in preparation for Chiang's expedition. Soon he used it to start a peasant revolution against Chiang. When Chiang's purge spread, Mao's revolution within a revolution began. Both revolutions were bloody because the situations were desperate. The peasant organization seized land and killed or publicly ridiculed the land-owners. Reporting on this time later, Mao said, "Revolution is not a dinner party, not a literary composition, nor a painting, nor a piece of pretty embroidery; it cannot be carried out softly, gradually, carefully, considerately, respectfully, politely, plainly, modestly." Perhaps he did not realize it but his wording was Confucian as well as poetic. He was still a strangely two-sided man.

From this time on, events stumbled over each other with dramatic speed. Mao tried to work with the Kuomintang government in Hankow. The Russian advisors that had been helping it were leaving but they told Mao that his revolution would have to go underground and depend entirely on peasant support and land reform.

Mao attempted revolts but they always seemed to fail. What was the best thing to do? Perhaps the Russians were right. He remembered the robber band in *All Men Are Brothers* and set up a mountain stronghold on the border between Hunan and Kiangsi Provinces. He chose a range called Chingkanshan with a circuit of about one hundred and fifty miles, an area covered with a heavy growth of bamboos and evergreens. Mist hung over it most of the year. It was a readymade fortress and refuge with only five roads leading in. Buddhist temples here and there were commandeered for quartering troops, for a hospital and for a printing press for Mao began to issue a paper almost at once. From October, 1927, until October 1934, the Red armies would find their hiding places in high mountains. Soviets were beginning to form in other places, but this army under Mao Tse-tung was the heart of the Chinese Communist movement. Sometimes Mao thought of one of the robber-bandits in his beloved novel who had had to choose between being eaten by a tiger and killing it. He killed it with his bare hands. Well, that was what *he* was going to have to do. Guerrillas would be his hands. He began to organize a guerrilla army. He worked out rules and orders. He wrote slogans. They rang out among the mist-covered mountains and would ring through China for many years.

> *When the enemy advances, we retreat.*
> *When he escapes, we harass.*
> *When he retreats, we pursue.*
> *When he is tired, we attack.*

The peasant army attacked Canton, but the attack failed. The army had to draw back to its mountains. Then in the spring of 1928 Chu Teh, the man who had been organizing a group of Chinese Communists in Germany, arrived at Chingkanshan with his men and joined Mao. They made a fine pair of leaders who were to stay together through all that lay ahead. During the year at Chingkanshan they led out in thirteen battles and fifty-seven small engagements. Some of their men wanted to try more massive things but Mao was learning from experience and he discouraged them. Chiang Kai-shek was still too strong. He had too much help. They would be wiped out by his well-armed troops. Mao's forces in the mountains were growing, too. His original 1,000 had been joined by Chu Teh's 2,000 and 8,000 more who had come of their own accord. Eleven thousand men were too many for the area to support. Food became very short. They had to move. They marched in to Kiangsi Province and started a soviet. They were ragged, dirty, sick, starved and far from hopeful looking but the Kiangsi peasants welcomed them because they were ready for revolt against a local government which had been corrupt for generations. During the year 1928, Mao's wife, the girl he had courted in Peking, lost her life in Chiang Kai-shek's purge. Mao's determination hardened even more.

The Kiangsi soviet became the main center of the Chinese Communists. In 1934, General Chiang attempted to encircle it with a blockade and squeeze it to death. He had tried to break the Communist power in four annihilation campaigns by now, and all had failed. This was his fifth and he was sure his last attempt but the Communists escaped from the Kiangsi encirclement and regathered to start a march to the northwest, 6,000 miles away. They had friends there, and there they could re-establish themselves.

Mao and Chu Teh led that dramatic march which took a year. Mao's second wife, a woman much younger than he who had gone to the same school as he had in Changsha, now marched with him though she was soon to have a child. They had two other children with them. That terrible march when Kuomintang planes strafed them from overhead, with desperate pushes, and hidings and frightful dangers made the going too hard for the children. The parents left them with peasants along the way. Mao's wife was struck by seventeen pieces of shrapnel. He was afraid she would die but she struggled on and he marveled at her courage. Later he said that the women of the march were braver than the men. When the baby was born, they left it, too, with peasants. When they could return years later, they tried to find the children but they could not discover a trace of any of them.

There is no full record of the Long March. About 85,000 men and 35 women began it. Mao was not only at the head, along with Chu Teh, he was now President of the Chinese Communist Government. One would not have thought it to see him. All he carried was a sun helmet, an old umbrella, a water bottle, a bowl for rice, a sweater and a knapsack on his back which was divided into compartments for maps, books, newspapers, and such things. He never wanted it out of his sight. Whenever they stopped to rest, or at night, he managed some kind of light to read captured documents and newspapers or to study maps.

General Chiang firmly believed that the Communist marchers would never be able to cross the Yangtze River which blocked their way. Even if they crossed it at the border of

Yunnan Province, they would still have to cross the impassable Tatu, a turbulent branch. They did both these things by ruse and by bare daring. When at last they reached Yenan, their destination in Shensi Province in the far northwest, their numbers had shrunk to 20,000 and many of these were new recruits who had joined along the way. The marchers had passed through eleven provinces, crossed rivers, negotiated snowy mountains and grass-covered quicksands. Several hundred thousand Kuomintang troops had tried to stop them, dozens of planes had strafed them, but they had survived.

General Chiang realized that his annihilation campaigns had failed to end the Communist power, but at least he had pushed the Reds out of the way. His mind was on other things for in 1937 Japan invaded China from the north. A young military man stationed near the Manchurian border, Chang Hsueh-liang, the Young Marshal, saw the invasion coming. The Communists who were beginning to move eastward saw it coming, too. The Young Marshal tried to alert General Chiang to the danger. Surely everyone had to join against Japan! He got nowhere. At last, in desperation he manoeuvred to have the General kidnapped to force him to cooperate. The whole country shuddered in surprise. General Chiang kidnapped! Impossible! At last the General made verbal promises and by September Communist and Kuomintang troops joined to form a massive force against the Japanese.

The two forces fought together until Japan surrendered under attacks of what became the Pacific Theater of World War II, in August, 1945. But everyone who really knew the situation realized that the Communists were doing the bitterest fighting in guerrilla warfare. Peasants were supporting them and many Nationalist troops were defecting to them. When Japan began to withdraw her forces under the terms of the defeat, the Communists moved in quickly to take over areas they had occupied. Civil war was at hand.

Mao's men rapidly pushed the Kuomintang forces back.

City after city fell and the Kuomintang government withdrew further and further into the interior until it reached the city of Chungking far up the Yangtze River above the gorges.

On October 1, 1949, the Communists took Peking. A great celebration was organized for the moment when Mao Tse-tung would proclaim the People's Republic of China. He stood on the balcony of the famous Gate of the Heavenly Peace (Tien An Men) where in centuries past tribute bearers from all over the world had made their way on their knees to the throne. Chu Teh was still beside him but when Mao began to speak he stepped back. It was Mao's moment.

Thousands of voices shouted, "May Mao Tse-tung live ten thousand years!" It was the age-old Chinese phrase used for emperors, but it showed the significance of the event being celebrated. An enormous flag with five yellow stars superimposed on a red field rose majestically and unfurled. Then the sea of human beings broke out in the song which had been sung by the Communist troops for twenty years and would be sung by generations of school children.

Arise, you who refuse to be slaves.
Our very flesh and blood will build a new Great wall.
A savage indignation fills us now,
Arise, arise, arise!

When the reverberating sound died down, a quiet Hunanese voice came over the loudspeaker, saying, "The Central Governing Council of the People's Government of China today assumes power in Peking."

A new dynasty had begun, but not the one dreamed of by the Kuomintang or the peoples of the West. The world looked on, suddenly afraid of the power of a revolution that could so move and change even China's millions, a full quarter of the earth's people.

12

1898–

Chou En-lai

PREMIER OF RED CHINA

None of Chou En-lai's classmates in Nankai Middle School (high school) in Tientsin, China, in the early 1900's would have dreamed that he was going to be a revolutionist. They would have found it even harder to suspect that he was going to be involved in a famous 6,000 mile march that the Chinese Communists made from central China to the northwest, or that he would have a price on his head, barely escape execution, and at last become one of the six men who ruled a quarter of the world's people.

They would not have connected him with any such roles because he came from a background that did not seem in the least revolutionary. His grandfather had held an important position in the Manchu Chinese Government in Peking, the monarchy that Chinese revolutionists wanted to overthrow. His father was famous as a scholar and as a teacher. Even Chou En-lai's mother was well-educated when this was unusual for women. Besides all this in his family, Chou En-lai was a fine student himself, and he looked the part of one. He had all the marks of a young gentleman of noble birth. He was only moderately tall, very slim and wiry, and he had such

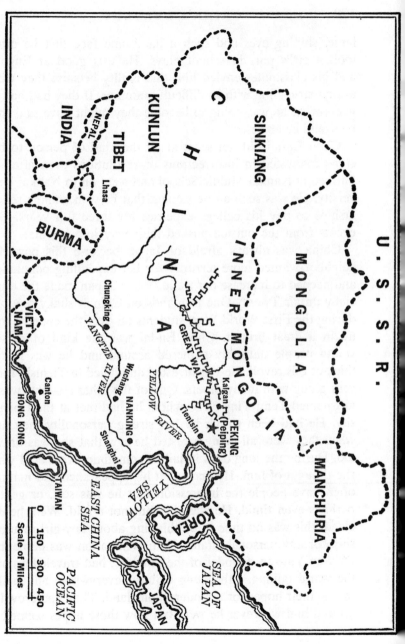

China Today

large, shining eyes and such a handsome face that he often took a girl's part in school plays. He was good at English and his classmates envied him that ability because they were always struggling with its difficult grammar. If they had had to guess what he was going to become they might have said that he would be an actor.

Chou En-lai did not seem at all the kind of person to become interested in insurrections or revolutions even after he finished at Nankai Middle School and went on to Nankai University. He was such a fine student that he won enough scholarships to pay his college expenses for three full years. But events from the outside pushed their way into his life.

China was always afraid of Japan because this powerful neighbor wanted more territory for her expanding population and needed to increase her trade. When Japan made the especially unfair Twenty-One Demands on China's shaky republic during the First World War, students all over the country rose up in a great protest. Chou En-lai was the kind of person young people naturally gathered around and he was in the thick of this revolt. He was arrested and jailed in Tientsin for a year along with many others. One of the other students was a girl named Teng Ying-ch'ao whom he had met at the University. He had been struck by her strong personality then and when they were all being arrested he saw that she was brave, too. During the long days in jail he sometimes wondered what she thought of him. He knew that his appearance and manner often gave people the impression that he was soft, or gentle, perhaps even timid. He was shy, but not afraid. Well, he decided, this was no time to be thinking about boy-girl relationships or any personal affairs. China's situation was desperate. Dr. Sun Yat-sen, founder of the republic, had traveled around the world talking with young Chinese everywhere and building up their hopes for a modern homeland. They had crowded around him wherever he went but now those hopes seemed to have failed. There would have to be another revolution, perhaps revolution after revolution.

As soon as Chou was released from jail, he set out for France. Many young Chinese had gone there to lead the labor battalions that China had sent to take part in the war or to interpret, or to study. To Chou France stood for change, for new ideas and for the best of European culture. Though he was a revolutionary, he loved the arts and he kept the tastes of a gentleman and a scholar.

Chou studied in France for two years. He learned to speak French and several other European languages fluently. While he was in Paris he took part, with other young Chinese revolutionists, in forming a Chinese Communist Party. Dr. Sun was accepting Communist help in the Chinese Revolution, so this was not strange. From France Chou En-lai went to England for several months and from there to Germany.

During these years abroad young Chou En-lai grew from a leader of student revolts into a mature and experienced revolutionary who began to gain a reputation for being a good organizer with a thorough understanding of politics. He kept a close contact with what was going on in China. He also carried on a correspondence with Teng Ying-ch'ao, the girl who had been arrested with him at Tientsin.

Chou En-lai was twenty-six when he returned to China in 1924. He was eager to take an active part in the Kuomintang or Nationalist Party which Dr. Sun had started, and in the Revolution which was still going on. For this reason he went to Canton where Nationalist activity was centered. Dr. Sun Yat-sen and Chiang Kai-shek, a young military leader who had just returned to the city after almost a year of military study in Moscow, were there. A new military school called the Whampoa Academy was being started in Canton and many Russians were on its staff. General Chiang Kai-shek was to lead a great expedition to Peking. Dr. Sun had dreamed of unifying Canton and Peking under the Nationalist Government, and had earlier attempted an expedition but it had failed. Now he counted on the brilliant young general to take Peking for the Revolution.

On the day that Chou En-lai and General Chiang Kai-shek first met, Chou entered the room and stood gracefully at ease before the stiff young militarist. Chou was not smiling because it would have been discourteous for him to do that, but he gave the impression of smiling because he was so apparently relaxed. General Chiang admired everything that was strictly disciplined from the time he was a boy, for he had always wanted to be a soldier. Now he guessed, if he did not already know from what he had heard, that Chou had just the opposite tastes.

General Chiang looked at Chou En-lai quickly and then motioned him to a guest chair. He could not keep from noticing that Chou's eyes were unusually striking. He saw, too, that in taking his seat, Chou had no military bearing at all. Instead, he looked like a young lord. Chiang realized uncomfortably that Chou's noble blood and his fine education put him in a position superior to his own. No matter what kind of work Chou undertook for the Revolution this would never be changed.

"The Kuomintang needs you at this time," General Chiang began, "for we have too few men who are trained in European languages and too few who understand our political plans." He watched Chou's face while he was speaking. It stayed easily pleasant.

"I am first of all a Revolutionist," Chou answered smoothly. "Whatever opportunities I have had should perhaps increase what I may be able to do for our country." He flecked a particle of dust from his fine European suit, and waited. He wanted to learn right away what his first assignment would be because he was sure that he would be put to work at once. He had already heard that the cadets in the new Academy had been wildly excited when they were told that he was coming to Canton.

"The position of chief of the political department at Whampoa Academy is vacant," General Chiang said. He had a staccato way of speaking that struck Chou as particularly impersonal. The General might as well have bombarded a stone wall with pebbles. Still, Chou waited. "I ask that you fill that position, at least for the time being. The Northern Expedition under my command will begin in a few months. The cadets must be thoroughly prepared and some must serve as officers." The General's eyes were as sharp and unblinking as Chou's were soft and alight with interest. Although neither man intended to show his secret feelings, Chou saw at once that the General disliked him, but because of a lack of qualified men, there was no one else General Chiang could ask to fill the Academy position.

"There will be other important duties to carry out once the Expedition starts," General Chiang continued, his abrupt tones giving no hint of the kinds of things he had in mind.

Chou En-lai simply nodded, saying to himself, "A militarist through and through. Who can guess what he is really thinking!" He glanced at the General fleetingly and then away again. "Does he really understand what the Revolution is about?" he asked himself. "Has Dr. Sun been able to get the basic reasons for it across to him?" Chou's friends argued that Chiang Kai-shek was not able to grasp their devotion to the idea of creating a modern, democratic China that would be recognized and respected internationally. Chou himself did not know. It was not a question he could answer yet.

Chou became chief of Whampoa Academy's political department and was flattered at the way the students welcomed him. In him the cadets had just the kind of man they wanted for he was well-educated, keen, committed to a new China, still with the air and breeding of a gentleman. They had been carefully chosen from among the most promising students all across China. Many came from wealthy or scholarly families. Chou En-lai won their respect and he also charmed them. When he married Teng Ying-ch'ao, the event added more color to the students' picture of him, for she, too, was a Revolutionist.

The Northern Expedition to Peking began in 1926. Dr. Sun had died unexpectedly the year before. General Chiang moved his forces northward toward Hankow, intending to go on to Peking from there. But a disagreement with the Kuomintang Government, now moved from Canton to Hankow, changed his plans drastically. First he sent orders to Chou En-lai. He was to go to Shanghai and prepare an insurrection so as to make it easier for the Nationalist forces to take the city when they arrived.

Chou was astonished at the orders. "I know something about Communism but I do not know how to go about planning and carrying through an insurrection," he told the handful of men who were with him. "The truth of it is that I have never had any military training at all." The Russian advisors who had been helping at the Academy had accompanied the Expedition to advise General Chiang, so they were not available. Now Chou half-smiled in the way characteristic of him and added, "Well, all the same we'll be on our way to the great city of Shanghai!"

Here he was, a young man who was altogether inexperienced in military methods, setting out to seize the international port. Of course, only the Chinese city and none of the concessions or areas granted to foreign countries, would be included in the objective.

When he reached Shanghai, Chou and his group planned to call a general strike at which time the workers would take over control of the city. In three months the local Communist Party which Chou headed organized 600,000 workers and the strike was called. It failed. Warlords in other parts of the country who owned the great businesses in the city held large interests in them heard what was going on and sent out orders to have some of the strike leaders beheaded. This was a method which usually ended any attempts to change things.

This first failure taught Chou En-lai a lesson. He knew now that plans had to be laid much more thoroughly and that strikers had to be carefully trained and well equipped if they were to succeed. He would need arms. He talked over plans with the labor leaders.

"We must have some expert marksmen and some Mausers for them," Chou announced. "These marksmen will be the hard core around which the others will be organized. Now how can we get weapons?"

"It is a question of smuggling," one of the men said. "There's no other way."

"How many can you get?"

"How many do you estimate we will need?"

"Let's say two hundred and fifty to three hundred."

"Three hundred at least."

"They will be found—and the marksmen will be trained."

"In the French Concession," they said almost in unison. The French Concession was famous as a haven for Revolutionists. Dr. Sun often went there. Chou laughed quietly and spoke a French phrase before he remembered that the others could not understand.

Not only were the three hundred hard-core men trained secretly in the French Concession but 2,000 special troops as well. These leaders then organized 50,000 pickets.

This time Chou En-lai felt satisfied with the preparations. The day the strike was to be called was approaching. It was in March, 1927, as General Chiang swung his Expeditionary forces down the Yangtze River Valley from Hankow toward Nanking. Shanghai would be next. Chou had enjoyed planning the strategy and he was confident and excited over what he now believed was going to be a great contribution to the Revolution. Helping the progress of the Expedition for the Nationalist Government also meant helping the Communist Party for Communists belonged to the Kuomintang and held high positions in it.

As the days of March passed, Chou En-lai sometimes remembered uncomfortably that the great strike was planned to help General Chiang take Shanghai. He could easily picture that cold mask-like face and he had trouble checking questions that kept coming to his mind. To what was General Chiang really committed? For what was he willing to die? Chou could not answer but he knew that there was nothing for him to do but to keep going forward.

Early on the morning of March 21 all of the industries of the great city of Shanghai shut down. Six hundred thousand well organized workers, five hundred of them armed, carried forward their plan. They seized the police stations, they took the arsenal and the garrison. Insurrectionists were promptly organized into an army and a citizens' government was proclaimed. Everything was going exactly as planned. The strike was a complete success. The city was ready for General Chiang to arrive and take it over.

"Accomplished!" Chou and his leaders said to each other, scarcely believing it themselves. "The city of Shanghai is captured for the Kuomintang!" Then one of the men looked at Chou with a peculiar expression and said softly, "Keep your eyes open, and your ears sharp, for the General does not like you." Chou only answered by raising his heavy brows. To himself he thought, "Then others, too, have my secret; a gnawing fear of this man who is leading the great Expedition. He is the one man in all of China that is most closely connected with the Revolution. Well, I need no warnings from anyone for I have my own fears to guide me."

General Chiang's troops reached the outskirts of Shanghai

and the triumphant workers handed the city over to them. Chou En-lai took part in the brief formalities. Would the General have anything to say to him and the other leaders of the insurrection—a word of commendation for an achievement carried through successfully by inexperienced men? "I do not care for myself," Chou said, "but I do care for the sake of others who worked with me. I've never had such cooperation before. They ought to be honored and repaid, for they took great risks."

Gradually news came that strange things had taken place in Nanking up the river. Some of Chiang's troops had sacked the city and attacked Europeans and Americans living there. The troops were identified as the General's men because of their Cantonese dialect. General Chiang at first hurriedly denied any responsibility for what had happened, then said Communist members of his troops had done it. When it was clear that he had to be responsible, he promised to carry out a great investigation. The incident raised suspicions and fears.

Shanghai was peaceful. No foreigners were bothered even though thousands of missionaries and traders had come to the port city to be safe from possible disturbances during the Expedition and the political unrest that followed. Gunboats and destroyers flying foreign flags had cast anchor in the broad mouth of the river near the city. But such precautions seemed unnecessary in spite of what had happened in Nanking.

Then on April 11, in the dead of night, a messenger came running on soft-soled shoes to Chou En-lai's quarters. A guard at the door slipped in silently and called to him in a toneless whisper. Chou seemed already wide awake. "Sir, the General has betrayed you. Escape, escape!"

Chou was on his feet instantly, drawing on his clothes. "Where did it begin—who?" he said in a low murmur.

"All over the city—a great massacre. Your name heads the list, sir."

Chou asked no more. "I might have known," he thought. "I hand him a victory—and now this!" A habitual, half-mocking smile touched his face though no one could see it in the darkness. He stepped out into the night and was quickly surrounded by his own men who had come at the news of danger.

He could not escape. General Chiang's Second Division captured him. Its commander ordered Chou's execution. "This is the honored end of a Revolutionist," Chou said to the others who had been seized with him. "We should not complain for it was the risk we knowingly took." He laughed in the insuppressible way he had. "After all, no one's neck can resist the blade of a well-sharpened sword, and no one's heart can turn a bullet," he went on in a philosophical mood. Some of the men could not bear his words now, and one dropped his head on his crossed arms and sobbed. "An insurrectionist knows that he is courting death, and a revolutionary has to accept the fact that he may not live to see the new day he dreams of. So, I am ready!" Chou told him quietly.

Day passed day and the execution was not carried out. Then one afternoon the second meal of the day was brought into the camp prison by a new soldier. The moment Chou saw him he knew that he was in disguise. It was not possible to talk with him but as he left he handed Chou a single page news sheet which was printed occasionally in the Second Division. Chou read it half-heartedly for it seldom had anything worth reading in it but as he did so he saw that here and there a character was lightly marked. When these were put together in a kind of sentence they seemed to say that the Second Division and the Whampoa Academy had something special in common. What sense did that make? It must be just the idle pencilling of some bored soldier. Yet he kept thinking of the two things, the Second Division and the Academy. Suddenly he remembered that the brother of the Second Division's commander who had ordered his execution, had been one of his students at the Academy. He had been a bright, loyal, young man. Could this man have some plan for his escape? He would wait and watch for any new signal. It turned out as he suspected. A few days later his former student manoeuvred his escape.

Chou En-lai had lost all hope that the Nationalists could bring China to a new day. He began now to lead a series of historic Communist efforts. These included a famous August First Uprising which laid the foundation for the organization of the Communist Army, the seizing of the great South China seaport, Swatow, and the dramatic and dangerous setting up of a Communist organization or commune in Canton. When this broke up because it was attacked so furiously by the Nationalists, Chou began to work through the Communist underground. He was wanted more than ever by the Nationalist Government which had established its new capital in Nanking and seemed to be flourishing under General Chiang.

But in 1931 Chou En-lai re-appeared in a Communist district in Kiangsi Province where the Reds were strong and well organized. He was appointed political counseller to General Chu Teh, Commander-in-Chief of the Red Army, the same man who had helped organize a Chinese Communist Party in Germany years before. Now Chou En-lai was an established leader of the Chinese Communists. They would amaze the world.

The Communist Army was ready to fight whether it had anything to fight with or not, and ready to die to the last man for what it had come to believe was China's only hope; a Communist way of life. In Kiangsi there was no seaport for the bringing in of supplies. Soldiers did not even have salt to flavor or preserve the meager food they could get from the local people who supported them in every way they could.

They were soon enclosed by a circle of highways and block

houses which General Chiang constructed around them, determined to at last put an end to the Communist guerrillas
who seemed never to be defeated. He had led one annihilation campaign after another trying to break their power, but
they always melted into the countryside, or defeated his men,
or worse still, won them over to their side and so got both
them and arms they badly needed. It was an embarrassing,
maddening situation for a man who considered himself, and
was thought of by others, as a particularly able military leader.
Perhaps he never actually thought of Chou En-lai personally
when he worried over the Kiangsi Communist center, but
Chou En-lai was still a man he would like to catch.

One of the most momentous events that followed came to
be known as the Long March. In 1934 the Reds slipped away
from their encircled center in Kiangsi and started a 6,000 mile
march toward the northwest. One night Chou En-lai, Chu Teh
and Mao Tse-tung held desperate counsel in a small town
where there was a ferry crossing to an upper branch of the
Yangtze called the Tatu River. They had to decide whether
men already on the other side of the river should try to join up
with them. The only way was over a famous bridge about one
hundred miles further on. A failure there would mean a de-
tour of three hundred miles. The men were so tired and weak
that few of them could survive the extra distance, even less the
constant strafing of General Chiang's pursuing planes. The
famous bridge was called The Bridge Fixed by Liu, an iron
chain suspension floored with boards. The Tatu River was a
rushing, roaring torrent full of gurgling whirlpools, pressed
between the walls of high gorges. Any crossing except by
bridge was impossible.

"The end will be the same whichever we decide," Chou said
at last. "If the men on the other side do not get over to us on
this side, they will be wiped out. If some get across, that many
will be saved and they may be enough to make it possible for

our full force to hold back the enemy so the march can continue." He was haggard, unshaven, scarcely recognizable.

The others turned to him thoughtfully. "You say there is no real choice, or if there is one, then it is to have the men try the crossing on The Bridge Fixed by Liu?" one asked slowly. "I too, see no other possibility."

The decision was made; the order given.

The men on the far side of the Tatu moved at night when the planes could not find them so easily. Occasionally the gleam of a torch signalled the Reds on the opposite shore that they were progressing. The path was hard to find. It led over dangerous precipitous rocks and through ravines formed by mountain torrents. When at last the company found the bridge, they discovered that half of the flooring on their side had been removed. Only bare chains reached to the midpoint, swinging out over the rushing stream in a terrifying motion. It was suicidal inching along hand over hand, while Nationalist guns waited to pick them off. But man after man swung down and moved slowly toward the boards that were left. The Nationalists had poured paraffin on the boards and hoped to set them afire. But the Reds came on. When they reached the floored section of the bridge they completed the crossing on their hands and knees. Some of them had dropped into the boiling stream below, but most got across. Their comrades roared out a welcome and rushed down to the bridge-head in such force, fighting so fiercely that the Nationalists ran for cover. Never had they seen such fiendish warfare as this!

When it was all over the Reds resumed their weary march. It seemed like an ancient tale of heroes. But they had gone through many events that seemed scarcely believable. Chou En-lai often put them into a setting of Chinese history and Mao Tse-tung said they reminded him of tales of a fictional band of robbers that he loved to read.

When the Long March was over, the Chinese Communists

strengthened themselves in their northwest haven. They were not thinking about the United States nor dreaming of the decisive part she was to play in the future of the Chinese people. True, America had long championed the Chinese in international affairs, sometimes for her own interests. Her first contact with fabulous Cathay had been made by traders who followed in the trail of British East India Company men. Then in the middle of the nineteenth century, Christian missionaries had become concerned for China's non-Christian peoples and for her having no up-to-date medical or educational institutions. In 1899, seeing that foreign powers were busily engaged in grabbing Chinese territory for themselves and their trade by means of special treaties and "spheres of interest," the United States had strongly supported what was called the Open Door Policy. Its purpose was to avoid having foreign countries partition China in any way they liked, to their own advantages, and to keep China open to economic development by all countries alike. John Hay, the United States Secretary of State at that time, put the full weight of his country behind this move and made it even stronger by getting promises from the foreign powers not to interfere with each other's trade, to allow the Chinese government to collect tariff from areas where they were active, and to agree that all foreign powers would pay equal harbor and railroad charges to the Chinese government.

The Open Door Policy gradually grew and changed so that it had two main purposes. The first was to save China from being divided among more powerful nations; the second was to give the powers that were developing investments there, equal treatment.

Of course the Chinese saw that while this measure helped them, it also helped the foreigners. Still, in the countryside, people often said, "But America is not an empire. She has no throne like we have. She does not take things by force like the

British. Americans are like us—they enjoy a joke—they play with the children." The Chinese students in the mission schools began to get new ideas about freedom and democratic forms of government. They were immensely attracted by them. Young Chinese began to dream. Dr. Sun Yat-sen was one of the dreamers.

As history moved on, the United States Government stood up for the Chinese people more than once. At the end of the First World War in the Washington Conference of 1921-22, it forced the expansion of the Open Door Policy through the Nine Power Treaty. Under the Kellogg-Briand Pact of 1928, Nanking was recognized as the seat of the Nationalist Government. When Japan seized Manchuria in 1931, the United States sent out the Lytton Commission to investigate what was going on.

Private individuals and foundations poured money into China to help the Chinese through terrible famines, and to forward medical and educational progress. Many of China's strongest revolutionary leaders, besides Dr. Sun Yat-sen, were men who had been trained in Westernized schools set up by Americans in great Chinese cities.

While Chou En-lai and other Communist leaders paused after the Long March, this background of Chinese-American relationships was probably not what they were thinking about. If it had been, they still would not have been able to foresee how events were going to entangle America and China. Japan was the one to bring it about.

When Japan had seized Manchuria in 1931 this was only a new step in her steady pressure on China. Chou En-lai had been one of the students thrown into jail when Japan had made her famous Twenty-one Demands years before. General Chiang's headstrong refusal to face Japan's threat instead of trying to wipe out the Chinese Communists by campaign after campaign, had led to the Long March. Now in 1936 the radical Communist government was strongly established in Yenan.

The situation with Japan was clearly desperate. The Communists talked things over among themselves and then offered to cooperate with General Chiang against Japan. He rejected their offer flatly. Chang Hsueh-liang, or the Young Marshal, who was in charge of Chinese troops from Manchuria, knew that his men were anxious to go out against Japan who was in their homeland instead of continuing to fight Communist Chinese. The Young Marshal decided to force the issue with the General. He arranged to have Chiang kidnapped en route to Sian, the Manchurian Army's headquarters.

"Look at the Young Marshal's demands," the men in Yenan said to each other. "They are just what we have been asking for! He is inviting our cooperation." Chou En-lai was in a curious spot. Soon he and the Red Army Chief of Staff were on their way to Sian to negotiate with General Chiang for a reorganization of the government into a Nationalist-Communist partnership, and an end to all civil war in favor of an all-out resistance to Japan.

It was no time for Chou to think of the past, but his memory of how he had almost lost his life in the Shanghai purge, could not be put down as he went on toward Sian with his military companion. Negotiations were tried for a week, the Generalissimo steadily refusing to grant the demands made upon him. Then Madame Chiang flew up from Nanking to join in the efforts and to beg her husband to take the food he had been refusing. On Christmas Eve General Chiang accepted the main points of the demands, and was released under most dignified and courteous arrangements. The whole event had given him world-wide publicity and personal support, and had dramatized how hard his position was.

Now that this hurdle had been passed, things began to happen quickly. Japan guessed that China was going to put up much greater resistance because of her new unity so she hastily moved forward into stronger military situations. The Chinese Communist and Nationalist leaders held almost constant conferences working out reorganization of their military forces under joint leadership. In the meantime, Japan moved further and further into China. On July 7, 1937, she brought about an incident at Marco Polo Bridge, near Peking, which became famous as the beginning of her open war on Chinese soil. By September of that year the Chinese forces were unified, the Communist now being called the Eighth Route Army of the National Revolutionary Army. This seemed fine, but Chou En-lai and the other Communist leaders knew that although this was a war of resistance against the common enemy, Japan, the real victory would be to the Chinese group that could appeal most strongly to the Chinese people's longing for nationalism.

The curious thing that happened was that as the war went on, Chinese leaders saw that the struggle that was taking place was really between Russia and Japan, for China. Each wanted her. The United States and other foreign nations stood back on the theory of being neutral and of not taking part in foreign wars. But America was deeply involved in trade with Japan and was at this very time sending her shiploads of scrap iron.

Japan attacked in the north and then at Shanghai. The great city fell after a brilliant defense by Chinese troops. As the Japanese pushed up the Yangtze River Valley, the Chinese capital moved from Nanking to Hankow, and at last on to Chungking. For several years things stood at a stalemate.

Fighting went on over the Chinese countryside. Communist Army men used guerrilla tactics. They won over the people where they passed and had their support in food and cover. The Nationalists used the more formal tactics in which General Chiang had trained them, taking stands which they tried to hold. They seemed to be the old-fashioned soldiers whom the Chinese had traditionally feared and scorned.

General Chiang felt sure that other powers were not going

to stand idly by and let Japan take over Asia, which she now declared to be her aim, without protesting. Japan believed she had the support of Germany, but the countries that General Chiang was thinking of were Russia and the United States. But developments in the Second World War now going on in Europe showed Japan that she could not count on any help from Germany because that country was too involved in Europe. Japan quickly signed a nonaggression pact with Russia.

The United States was beginning to be anxious about what Japan was doing in the Far East even though the Americans wanted desperately not to be involved in military operations there or in the Second World War at all. When France fell, Japan occupied Indo-China in her place. In July, 1941, the United States froze all Japanese assets in America. It was now clear that Japan and the United States were confronting each other hostilely. Secretary of State Cordell Hull attempted frantic negotiations with the Japanese envoys who came to Washington. But on December 7, 1941, Japan bombed the United States installations in Pearl Harbor, Hawaii. The United States was thrown into military partnership with China against Japan. The United States had demanded steps of Japan that were direct and drastic, and had left no face-saving way open for negotiation. The war in the Pacific began.

America was now deeply involved in China's war, but she hoped to keep China fighting and making the invader pay a heavier and heavier price. General Chiang, who was heading up both the Nationalist and the Communist forces, had rather different aims. He wanted to enhance China's prestige abroad, and make sure that the Nationalists kept the upper hand at home. He asked American for enormous sums of money to build up his forces and armaments. He was dismayed when the American military leaders decided to establish a China-Burma-India Theater of War, because all China's seaports were in enemy hands, and made him head only of the China Theater.

We do not know that anyone had a chance to see Chou En-lai's expression when this plan was put into operation. He felt it would never work because he understood General Chiang. The financial help that poured in all passed through the Nationalist Government, which was the recognized government, and General Chiang made sure that the Nationalist interests were served.

Chou En-lai and the other Communist leaders could not help but see that well-intentioned American help was working against Chinese unity because all of it went to the Nationalists. And the Nationalists were not really putting their hearts into fighting even though gallant and able Americans like Lieutenant General Joseph W. Stilwell, General Albert C. Wedemeyer, Ambassador Patrick A. Hurley, and at last General George C. Marshall all tried to inspire, or badger, or mediate among the Chinese leaders so as to get the war against Japan moving.

Chou En-lai going in and out of Chungking, the wartime capital of Free China, saw that the war would never be waged from that center. "The Americans are unwilling to believe that General Chiang wants others to fight the war for him," he often thought. America's problem was that she could not build up the Nationalist military strength with money and arms and at the same time upset it politically by demanding more democratic methods and cooperation with the Chinese Communists.

When Japan was at last defeated by the all-out effort of Western forces in the Pacific, and V-J Day, August 14, 1945, came, it was still not to be the end of American help to China. The Communist leaders saw that America was caught. There was nothing she could do but recognize and help General Chiang's government. Hope of unity was completely gone now. The Communist forces quickly moved into the areas

vacated by the withdrawing Japanese armies. A new phase of
the Communist-Nationalist civil war was beginning. The
United States was committed to go on standing by the Generalissimo. She would have to go on pouring millions of her
dollars into trying to support a sinking Nationalist economy
and providing arms for a halfhearted Nationalist army.

In this curious way, history made Russia and Communism
the only hope of the Chinese people. They were thoroughly
disillusioned by the leadership which had claimed to be following the dream of Dr. Sun Yat-sen. At the same time, the
Americans seeing the threat and danger that Communism was
to a democratic way of life, drew back, unwilling to recognize
the Communist regime.

The Communist Government in Peking enjoyed its success
and its inheritance of history. Its parades moved through the
ancient streets. Chou En-lai became one of the new government's leading men. He was appointed Premier and went all
over the world representing his country. He still speaks beautiful English and French as well as German and Russian. He is
hard at work as one of Red China's most prominent leaders,
her ablest and best-known ambassador to the outside world.
At heart he is still a Revolutionary and ever-ready to win new
countries to Communist ideas. Diplomats do not have to
guess at what is going on behind his suave expression and the
eyes that still glow beneath their heavy brows.

Bibliography

Berkov, Robert H., *Strong Man of China*. Cambridge, Massachusetts, The Riverside Press, 1938.

Buck, Pearl S., *Imperial Woman*. New York, The John Day Company, 1956.

────── *Tell the People*. New York, The John Day Company, 1945.

Chen, Stephen and Payne, Robert, *Sun Yat-Sen: A Portrait*. New York, The John Day Company, 1946.

Chiang Kai-shek, General and Madame, *General Chiang Kai-shek*. Garden City, New York, Doubleday, Doran and Company, Inc., 1937.

Clubb, O. Edmund, *Twentieth Century China*. New York, Columbia University Press, 1962.

deBary, William Theodore, *Sources of Chinese Tradition*. New York, Columbia University Press, 1960.

Fairbank, John King, *The United States and China*. New York, The Viking Press, 1962.

Giles, Herbert A., *A History of Chinese Literature*. New York, D. Appleton & Company, 1928.

Grousset, Réné, *The Rise and Splendour of the Chinese Empire*. Berkeley and Los Angeles, University of California Press, 1953.

Hahn, Emily, *Chiang Kai-shek*. Garden City, New York, Doubleday and Company, 1955.

Kaizuka, Shigeki, *Confucius*. (The Ethical and Religious Classics by Earl and West, No. 17) New York, The Macmillan Company, 1956.

Ku, Pan and members of his family, intended as continuation of Ssu Ma Ch'ien's famous history, 32-92 A.D. (in Chinese), *History of the Former Han Dynasty.*

Lin, Yutang, *The Importance of Living.* New York, The John Day Company, 1937.

Payne, Robert, *Portrait of a Revolutionary.* New York, Abelard-Schuman, 1961.

———— *The Revolt of Asia.* New York, The John Day Company, 1947.

Sharman, Lyon, *Sun Yat-Sen, His Life and Its Meaning.* New York, The John Day Company, 1934.

Snow, Edgar, *Red Star Over China.* New York, Random House, Inc., 1938.

———— *The Other Side of the River.* New York, Random House, Inc., 1961.

White, Theodore H. and Jacoby, Annalee, *Thunder Out of China.* New York, William Sloane Associates, Inc., 1946.

Yu-chang, Wu, *The Revolution of 1911.* Printed in the Peoples' Republic of China, 1961.

THE AUTHOR

CORNELIA SPENCER, who was born and raised in China, brings to this book a real interest in the Chinese people and a sound background for writing about them. Miss Spencer did her college work in the United States, after which she returned to China and did not leave there to settle in America until 1935. She now lives in Bethesda, Maryland. Miss Spencer's main interest has been in factual books for young people, although she has also published novels. Many of her books have been about Eastern countries—China, Japan, the Philippine Islands and India. She has written a number of biographies of interesting personalities—the Soong sisters, Prime Minister Nehru, Ambassador Carlos Romulo, former President Harry Truman, and Pearl Buck.